How to Be Successful in Your First Year of Teaching High School:

Everything You Need to Know That They Don't Teach You in School

By Anne Kocsis

HOW TO BE SUCCESSFUL IN YOUR FIRST YEAR OF TEACHING HIGH SCHOOL: EVERYTHING YOU NEED TO KNOW THAT THEY DON'T TEACH YOU IN SCHOOL

1405 SW 6th Avenue • Ocala, Florida 34471 • Phone 800-814-1132 • Fax 352-622-1875
Web site: www.atlantic-pub.com • E-mail: sales@atlantic-pub.com
SAN Number: 268-1250

Library of Congress Cataloging-in-Publication Data

Kocsis, Anne B., 1965-
How to be successful in your first year of teaching high school : everything you need to know that they don't teach you in school / by Anne B. Kocsis.
p. cm.
Includes bibliographical references and index.
ISBN-13: 978-1-60138-335-8 (alk. paper)
ISBN-10: 1-60138-335-5 (alk. paper)
1. First year teachers--Training of--United States. 2. Language arts (Secondary)--United States. 3. Teacher effectiveness--United States. I. Title.
LB2844.1.N4K63 2010
373.11--dc22

2010016890

PEER REVIEWER, ASSISTANT PROJECT MANAGER: Marilee Griffin
INTERIOR DESIGN: Holly Marie Gibbs • INTERIOR LAYOUT: Samantha Martin
COVER DESIGN: Jackie Miller • millerjackiej@gmail.com

Printed in the United States

Printed on Recycled Paper

We recently lost our beloved pet "Bear," who was not only our best and dearest friend but also the "Vice President of Sunshine" here at Atlantic Publishing. He did not receive a salary but worked tirelessly 24 hours a day to please his parents. Bear was a rescue dog that turned around and showered myself, my wife, Sherri, his grandparents Jean, Bob, and Nancy, and every person and animal he met (maybe not rabbits) with friendship and love. He made a lot of people smile every day.

We wanted you to know that a portion of the profits of this book will be donated to The Humane Society of the United States. *–Douglas & Sherri Brown*

The human-animal bond is as old as human history. We cherish our animal companions for their unconditional affection and acceptance. We feel a thrill when we glimpse wild creatures in their natural habitat or in our own backyard.

Unfortunately, the human-animal bond has at times been weakened. Humans have exploited some animal species to the point of extinction.

The Humane Society of the United States makes a difference in the lives of animals here at home and worldwide. The HSUS is dedicated to creating a world where our relationship with animals is guided by compassion. We seek a truly humane society in which animals are respected for their intrinsic value, and where the human-animal bond is strong.

Want to help animals? We have plenty of suggestions. Adopt a pet from a local shelter, join The Humane Society and be a part of our work to help companion animals and wildlife. You will be funding our educational, legislative, investigative and outreach projects in the U.S. and across the globe.

Or perhaps you'd like to make a memorial donation in honor of a pet, friend or relative? You can through our Kindred Spirits program. And if you'd like to contribute in a more structured way, our Planned Giving Office has suggestions about estate planning, annuities, and even gifts of stock that avoid capital gains taxes.

Maybe you have land that you would like to preserve as a lasting habitat for wildlife. Our Wildlife Land Trust can help you. Perhaps the land you want to share is a backyard—that's enough. Our Urban Wildlife Sanctuary Program will show you how to create a habitat for your wild neighbors.

So you see, it's easy to help animals. And The HSUS is here to help.

2100 L Street NW • Washington, DC 20037 • 202-452-1100
www.hsus.org

Acknowledgements

"Writing is an exploration. You start from nothing and learn as you go."

— Edgar Lawrence Doctorow, American author and professor (1931 — Present)

I am extremely lucky to have an opportunity to teach and learn while I do what I love most — writing. This book is dedicated to my wonderful friends and family who constantly help me navigate the never-ending challenges in my daily life. I would like to offer special thanks to Kathy Heisler and Michelle Sharp for helping me compile sources to interview while my son was in the hospital. Additionally, I want to thank my editor, Kim Fulscher, whose patience and advice continues to help me become a better writer. Above all, I wish to thank my children for teaching me what is important every single day. John, Matt, and Katie: I love you; you are my inspiration!

Table of Contents

Foreword

Becoming a high school teacher is possibly the scariest and yet most rewarding of jobs, next to parenting. In a way, you are a surrogate parent to your students, sometimes spending more time with most of them than their biological parents and/or care-giving guardians, and influencing them in ways those adults can or do not. I congratulate the author, Anne Kocsis, for addressing the real issues — from preparing a viable résumé to handling difficult parents to celebrating your career choice. Kocsis presents the good, the bad, and the ugly when it comes to teaching in today's high schools — thankfully, she also presents ways to address and master the good, the bad, and the ugly. As high school teachers, we encounter all three every day.

Teaching in American high schools is tricky business. And, as is so sadly but accurately stated at the start of Section I, the dismal survival rates for high school teachers could spur their own distressing reality show, depicting the tears and frustrations of those teachers who don't make it. But the case studies in this book, along with my personal promise, are evidence to the contrary; proving that teaching at the high school level is one of the most gratifying and satisfying careers out there. We often get to teach what we know and love to students who need us and who, upon leaving our classrooms, will invariably miss and thank us.

This book will be your guide through your first year teaching high school. You will learn about discipline in the classroom, how to create lesson plans, where to go for mentoring and advice, and everything you wanted to know about the different types of schools available. Most importantly, this book will show you how to be the best role model possible — the one who upholds high moral standards, always uses proper grammar, shuns slang, and eschews teen talk. Keep this in mind: good behavior often equals "smart" in the minds of high schoolers.

After reading this book and acing your first year, students will *thank* you for your hard work, your passion, and your high standards. They will someday go to higher learning institutions and to work, and they will remember you and all you taught them — the way you made them accountable for themselves, their words, their actions, and their work. When you made them submit homework assignments, take grueling tests, write research papers, and perform difficult laboratory experiments, they will remember that you never let them slide, in or out of the classroom. They will realize how proud you were of them. These things stick. Your high school students will become better people, in part because of you.

I thank you for making the tough but smart choice to become a high school teacher, and I wish you only the very best. As Anne Kocsis says at the start of Chapter 12, "...you have no idea what you have gotten yourself into." Nevertheless, I hope you never want to get out.

Cheers!

Colleen Brogan
English teacher
Supervisor

Author's Note

"Learning is finding out what we already know. Doing is demonstrating that you know it. Teaching is reminding others that they know just as well as you. You are all learners, doers, and teachers."

— Richard Bach, American author (1936-Present)

Compiling this book has been a great process for me. Throughout different stages of my life, I have filled many of the roles discussed in the book. I have been a child and a student. I have been an employee and a boss. I have been a parent, a teacher, a coach, and an aide. I have also acted in the capacity of nurse and counselor due to circumstances that exist in my life.

Although my degree is in English and not in education, I have taken a number of education courses over the years. I also spent some time working in the Cumberland Valley school district in Mechanicsburg, Pennsylvania. Additionally, I studied learning styles and have used the information with students and within my own family. I have three very different children; they are all bright in their own way, and they each have their own specific challenges. We have navigated gifted and other special-needs issues. We have handled medical problems, academic and non-academic dilemmas, and administrative issues. Each day, I continue to learn more about children, learning, teaching, and the challenges facing today's school systems.

My children are each a blessing, a gift, and an inspiration to me. Their individual challenges have taught me more than any of my own work experiences. As I write this book, my two sons are already teenagers maneuvering the daily pressures present in secondary school, and my daughter is not far behind. Additionally, my middle child has spent more time in the hospital than in the classroom this school year. If I could impart one bit of wisdom to you, it is this: you can get through anything in life as long as you have a good sense of humor!

As Confucius once said, "a journey of a thousand miles begins with a single step." This is just the first step in a new adventure. I hope the information I have compiled here assists you in your own journey to teach and inspire others.

Introduction

"Teaching is the highest form of understanding."

— Aristotle, Greek philosopher (384 BC-322 BC)

Congratulations! You have taken the most important step by making a decision concerning what you kind of work you want to do. You have decided to become a high school teacher. The next question is: Where are you in the process of making it a reality? Did you go to college with that goal in mind? If you are a college graduate in possession of an education degree, you have taken the traditional approach to becoming a teacher. In that case, this book is full of tips and advice for someone just like you.

But wait! What if you did not go to college specifically to become a high school teacher? What if you went to college for another purpose, graduated with a four-year degree, but have since changed your mind on the career path you want to pursue? What if you are a mother or father who stayed home to raise children and are now in search of a job that coincides with the children's school schedule? Perhaps you have already had at least one career, and want to change paths for some other personal reason. In any case, this book is for you too.

In the pages that follow, you will find information on the various routes to becoming a teacher, from a four-year education degree to the mid-career guest teacher path, and everything in between. It includes advice on student teaching, substitute teaching, writing your résumé, and preparing for the job interview. Additionally, there are reports to help you determine where you want to seek employment. There are case studies and charts concerning the multitude of secondary schools in the United States, including public, private, and cyber. There is also information on pay scales and the different types of environments surrounding these schools, all compiled to assist you in your job pursuit.

Once you have a job, there will be a host of other challenges to face. Teaching is a very rewarding profession, but it can also be very stressful, especially for a new teacher. Teaching high school is particularly overwhelming. In addition to the pressures of a new job, new high school teachers need to work with people who may not want to be there: teenagers. Therefore, this book will help you adapt to your environment quickly and effectively. It discusses the steps you took and information you gathered in preparation to become a teacher, and adds practical information from numerous sources currently working in the modern high school setting. The combination will provide you with all of the pertinent information necessary for a navigating a successful first year in this profession.

This book will not only help you navigate through your the first year as a new teacher, it will also help you prepare to become a great high school teacher in the years to come. It provides pages of advice on dealing with difficult people and challenging situation. It also offers insight into what to expect in regards to extra responsibilities and professional development in the years that follow.

Many experienced teachers were interviewed to compile this information. The book is filled with the answers to the most commonly asked questions, along with tips and suggestions on handling a wide array of challenges facing high school teachers today. Hopefully, this is just the first step in a long, successful, and very rewarding career.

Section 1:

I Want to Teach High School — Now What?

"Education is the most powerful weapon which you can use to change the world."

— Nelson Mandela,
former president of South Africa (1918-Present)

What exactly does it mean to be a teacher? First and foremost, to teach is to impart knowledge and wisdom upon someone else. That is the obvious part, but teaching is really so much more. With technological advances, such as the Internet, information about the world is so much more accessible. A good teacher must also know how to use and impart knowledge responsibly. They must also take into account the differences in their students. Teaching a student who wants to learn is one thing, but inspiring a student to want to learn is another.

In the early years of the new millennium, there was a shortage of teachers in our country. Now, more individuals than ever before are seeking employment in this profession. Some are right out of college, while others are professionals seeking a change in career. Regardless of where you fall in that spectrum, there are teacher jobs available if you take the time to research what is out there. Before you start applying for jobs, however, you must be prepared. There are certain requirements for secondary school teachers.

This section addresses the educational and paperwork requirements necessary for being eligible to teach high school in the United States. It also discusses the wide array of secondary school working environments to help you find the right fit for your personality. Finally, it offers tips for getting experience, putting together a résumé, and interviewing successfully to get the job you seek.

Chapter 1

Various Paths and Preparation

"Do not go where the path may lead; go instead where there is no path and leave a trail."

— Ralph Waldo Emerson, American essayist and poet (1803-1882)

In 1794, a group in New York City known as the Society of Associated Teachers established the first recognized teacher requirements. City officials organized the association to create uniform teacher qualifications in the city. Eleven years later, a group called the Free School Society was the first to secure public funds to pay for teacher courses. It was not until 1885, however, that a college preparatory course was developed by Brown University. Now, more than a century later, all teachers have to undergo some form of training in order to become certified and licensed to teach. There are many different ways to receive the necessary training, but ultimately all full-time secondary teachers in the United States are expected to have all of the following:

- Bachelor's degree
- Student teaching experience
- Teacher certification
- Teacher's license

These are the basic requirements. There are exceptions. For example, if you are seeking employment in a private school, you still need a bachelor's degree, but you do not need a license. Obviously, if you have fulfilled the requirements above, you will have more job opportunities to choose from.

The United States currently employs approximately 6.2 million teachers. There are some areas of the country experiencing a glut in the teacher market; others still have difficulty filling teacher positions. Additionally, there is a big problem with attrition in this industry. According to the Web site **www.retainingteachers.com**, the National Commission on Teaching and America's Future (NCTSF) cite that approximately one-third of all new teachers leave by the end of their first three years and virtually 50 percent quit within five years. In other words, there is always a need for good new teachers who are enthusiastic. Just as there are numerous types of teachers, there are multiple ways to get to this point. If you know you want to be a teacher, and have not yet received the necessary training, here are some of the ways to accomplish your goal:

- Traditional route
- Professional Development School (PDS)
- Part-time traditional route
- Internet degree option
- Fast track programs
- Continuing education
- Guest teacher program

The Traditional Route

The traditional route to becoming a high school teacher is to attend a four-year college, major in education, and obtain a bachelor's degree. Many younger teachers start out this way. By attending college right out of high school and majoring in education, you will be able to take all of the courses you need. If you know from the start that you want to teach in a secondary school, you will need to major in the subject you wish to teach. Each school has its own list of core accreditation requirements, but most expect aspiring teachers to take technology courses to keep up with the changing trends. These programs include student teaching and preparing for certification and licensure exams, and are accredited by the National Council for Accreditation of Teacher Education (NCATE) and the Teacher Education Accreditation Council (TEAC). One of the main advantages of this method is the school guidance and assistance in all of these areas.

The benefits of NCATE accreditation

If go decide to go the traditional route, consider attending a university that has been sanctioned by the NCATE. Professionals in the education field have reviewed these schools. Additionally, the programs maintain higher standards for students recommended for certification and licensure. This is a benefit when you are first looking for a job and do not have a lot of experience on your résumé. Additionally, it may make it easier to get a job in another state. Each state has its own licensure requirements, but many states have agreements with NCATE-accredited schools that simplify the licensing process.

Professional Development Schools (PDS)

Another option for individuals who have already earned a bachelor's degree is a professional development school (PDS) program, now offered in many states. These programs exist through partnerships between universities and specific schools. The one-year programs expedite the process by merging theory with practice. They allow students to experience a full year of teaching, with guidance and supervision. Individuals interested in these programs must apply through the university partnering with the secondary school.

Part-time Traditional Route

Even if you are not right out of high school, you can still take the traditional route. Many colleges offer night classes for individuals who are working their way through school. Consider taking one or two courses at a time until you obtain your education degree. If you already have a bachelor's degree in something else, particularly if it is in the subject you wish to teach, you are almost there. In order to teach in a public school, you may only need a limited number of additional credits in education, plus student teaching in order to receive certification. Additionally, there may be other job opportunities available outside of the public school system. Some private schools do not require an education degree from their teachers, providing they have bachelor's degrees in a relevant subject matter.

Internet Degree Option

Online classes are available in virtually any subject. You can complete your education degree, take courses that enable you to specialize in a specific subject area, or further your education by this method. Once you determine what you want to teach, you can research what you kind of classes you need in order to accomplish your goal. In searching for online teaching programs, you will find numerous schools offering teacher certification programs through online classes. To assist you in sifting through the information, start by visiting a Web site, such as **www.earnmydegree.com**. It posts links to a multitude of schools organized by area of interest, making it easier to find a program to fit your needs.

Fast Track Programs

Many individuals are deciding to become teachers as a second career. According to the U.S. Department of Education, the number of new teachers that enter the field right out of college has significantly decreased over the last two decades. Instead, many new teachers are those who have other career and life experiences prior to entering this profession. One organization that helps place these mid-career individuals into teaching jobs is the New York Teaching Fellows. They have assisted more than 9,000 career-changing individuals with securing teaching jobs in the city.

Since there is a shortage of certain types of teachers, in some areas of the country, there are some accelerated teaching programs developed to fill specific needs. For example, in June 2009, Governor Ed Rendell of Pennsylvania set up a fast-track program to address the shortage in qualified secondary math and science teachers. The state program allows mid-career professionals with a bachelor's degree to complete a four-month teacher-training course, instead of the traditional four-year education degree program. There are a variety of fast-track alternative teacher training courses in the United States. Other programs include, but are not limited to, the following:

- **Troops to Teachers** — Individuals retired from the various branches of service are eligible to begin second careers as teachers in public schools.

- **Teach for America** — Recent college graduates attend summer sessions sponsored through private, corporate, and government donations. Subsequently, they commit to teaching in rural and low-income urban areas for at least two years.

- **The New Teacher Project (TNTP)** — Fee-for-service organization that recruits, trains, and prepares select individuals to teach in shortage-area subjects and high-needs schools.

Continuing Education

Some schools, such as many private schools, will accept teachers without education certification as long as they have a bachelor's degree in the subject they are teaching. Additionally, if there is an immediate need for a teacher, some schools may allow you to teach under these circumstances while you are finishing up your education degree. This is not permitted in the public school system.

Guest Teacher Program

There is a huge need for high school substitute teachers. There are two- to three-day programs available that provide expedited training to quickly increase the pool of available substitute teachers. In Pennsylvania, the Intermediate Unit offers this program and trains individuals who can substitute in 27 different school districts. This is a good way to get into the school district. You can make money, build your credentials, and decide if you want to become a full-time teacher. It is also a great, highly flexible alternative if you only want to work part-time. If you decide you want to a full-time high school teacher, you can finish your credentials and become certified. If you do not enjoy teaching at this level, you have saved yourself time and money. Not everyone is cut out to be a high school teacher.

Certification and Licensure

Regardless of the path you take to become a teacher, you will need to fulfill certain other requirements before seeking employment in this field. In order to be eligible to teach in the public school system, you must first be certified. Since every state has different certification and licensure requirements, it is best to research the licensing regulations in the area you wish to teach in. The type of certification required varies from state to state. It also depends on the age level and subject you are planning to teach. In order to gather the specific requirements for each state, you can check with the state board of education. Information on who to contact is available online. For specific information on the certification requirements in your state, check the current information compiled by the U.S. Department of Education in the Education Resources Organization Directory (EROD).

To do so, visit the following Web site: **www2.ed.gov/erod**. When you get to the page, look for the box titled "simple search" and type in "state education agency." You will be directed to a list of all of the boards of education, listed alphabetically by state. There is a Web link at each state name. There is also a URL link and an e-mail address for a contact person for each organization. To research certification information online, type in the state name and the words "board of education" in the search engine on your computer. State specific certification details are also available at the Certification Map Web site: **www.certificationmap.com**. Simply click on the state in which you wish to seek employment.

Determine the school district you want to work in and research their certification requirements. This may save you a lot of time, allowing you to start working much more quickly in this chosen field. All districts are listed on The United States Department of Education's Web site. This can be found at **www.ed.gov**. The National Center for Education Statistics Web site includes information about each district in the country; visit **www.nces.ed.gov**. Hover the cursor over the "School, College, & Library Search" tab at the top and click "Search for Public School Districts." The Web site will provide the district name and contact information for all districts in that state.

According to law, anyone hired as a full-time public school teacher in any of the 50 United States and the District of Columbia must also have a teacher's license. Private school teachers, on the other hand, do not need to have a license to teach. Each State Board of Education has its own licensure advisory committee and each state has its own specific regulations. For example, in Pennsylvania, to apply for a secondary school license, you must have at least a 3.0 GPA in your major. In some states, such as Massachusetts and New York, a master's degree is required for licensure. In other states, a master's degree may be required for professional development or for administrative positions of principal or higher. The following requirements, however, are standard licensure requirements in the United States:

- Bachelor's degree
- Completion of approved teaching training program
- Completion of supervised student teaching
- A passing grade on The Praxis Series™ test

The Praxis Series was created by the Educational Testing Service™ (ETS). It is a series of assessments that most states use to certify teachers and provide them with the necessary license to teach. There are two different tests in the series that you may need to take for the jobs you are seeking. They are:

- **Praxis ISM** — This is a test that measures basic knowledge and skills, such as reading, writing, and math. These are the basic areas required for entry into most teacher education programs.

- **Praxis IISM** — This is a test that assesses more specific subject matter knowledge. This is a requirement for teacher licensure in 39 out of the 50 Unites States.

Like any other test, being prepared provides the best chance for success. The ETS has study aids and practice tests available at their Web site, located at **www.ets.org/praxis**.

The degree, student teaching observations, and test scores are all evaluated for licensure. Licenses are then granted as follows:

- Early childhood (preschool through third grade)
- Elementary (first through sixth grade, but may include up to eighth grade in some states)
- Middle school (fifth through eighth grades)
- Secondary school — by subject matter (seventh through twelfth grades)
- Special subject — such as art and music (kindergarten through twelfth grade)

Background Checks

Find out the laws regarding working with children in your area. In order to work with children in any capacity, either as a paid employee or a volunteer, you must undergo certain background checks. If you have not already done so, the school will require you do acquire a number of clearances before you can start working. Check with individual school districts and employers to determine their specific requirements. You will incur a cost for each application. Ask to see if the organization reimburses for the cost. Some do, but most do not. The following is a basic list of the types of clearances required by schools:

- State criminal background check
- Federal criminal background check, including fingerprinting
- Child abuse clearance

The information is checked against state police and FBI databases. The program searches for past criminal activity and any history of child abuse. The current system evolved from a series of government actions. They are: the National Child Protection Act of 1993 (NCPA), the Violent Crime Control Act of 1994, and the Volunteers for Children Act (part of the Crime Identification Act of 1998). Federal laws mandate these background checks.

Additionally, schools require proof of a recent tuberculosis (TB) test with negative results. Many colleges also recommend that students entering into their student teaching internship obtain professional liability insurance. Some universities make it mandatory to purchase it before they are allowed to enter into their student teaching. Student teaching liability insurance provisions offer protection in civil legal matters. Most of these policies cover issues such as negligence, libel, grading disputes, and student injury. Since the student teachers are not paid, they are considered volunteers; therefore the school they are teaching at does not cover them with their insurance. There are sources for students to get a policy at a student rate, from the state education association and other sources. Information explaining how to apply for this insurance appears in all student teacher handbooks.

Acquiring Teaching Experience

As you apply for jobs, you will be questioned about your teaching experience. For most new teachers, the experience that immediately comes to mind is their student teaching internship. If you plan to teach in the public school system, student teaching is a critical endeavor, as it is a requirement for licensure. Given its importance, you need to make the most of the experience right from the beginning.

Student teaching

A student teacher is student at a college or university working toward the completion of his or her education degree. The student teacher internship is completed during the final semester of study. Depending on the university, student teachers may be required to gain field experience in multiple settings. In other words, they may need to perform student teaching in urban and suburban schools. Most student teachers must also teach in two different classrooms and be observed or supervised by two separate teachers, known as cooperating or "co-op" teachers.

"When I did my student teaching, the great advice my cooperating teacher gave me that has proven to be correct was, 'You must expect great things out of students. Sometimes you may only get mediocre, but you sometimes get great — but if you expect mediocre, you will get nothing.'"

— Donna Benson, teacher,
Cumberland Valley High School

Every college has its own distinct manner for handling the student teaching portion of the curriculum. Despite a few simple variations, they are all relatively similar. Each college has its own student teaching handbook. The guidebooks may also contain school or state-specific information, such as forms for certification and licensure.

Despite variations, the student teaching handbooks all address the following:

- Defined terms of the student teaching assignment
- Goals for the student teacher

- Performance evaluation items
- Responsibilities and expectations

Each program covers the same elements, despite the differences in the program structure or wording. For example, the University of Miami divides their student teaching program into four basic phases:

Weeks 1-2: Induction Phase — Observation, participation, and assisting

Weeks 3-4: Initial Teaching Phase — Assume responsibility for teaching lessons

Weeks 5-15: Full Teaching Phase — Gradually assume full teaching load, as much as allowed

Week 16: Concluding Phase — Phase out of instructional activities and observe other school areas

For secondary schools, student teachers spend at least two full days per week in the classroom.

The student teaching assignments vary. Students planning to teach in a secondary school environment may be observed by multiple supervisors. There will be a student teacher supervisor who reviews the following domains:

- Planning and preparation
- Classroom environment
- Instructional delivery
- Overall professionalism

Additionally, there will be some form of subject-specific observation. This evaluation consists of the following areas of assessment:

- Grasp of the subject
- Instructional delivery
- Evaluation of lesson plans

"When you go to observe a teacher, do not focus solely on the lesson and how it is implemented. Instead, place your focus on how they control the classroom environment. When the bell rings, are students seated or all over the place? Does the teacher just call on students randomly, expecting an answer, or do they call on volunteers? How does the teacher refocus students who are not paying attention? Pay attention to these subtleties of classroom management, because it is these minor details that need to be in place before you worry about creating effective lessons."

— Michael Lutz, world cultures teacher, Cumberland Valley High School

Depending on the program, you may need to submit a video of yourself in the classroom and written reports on assigned topics related to the student teaching semester. In addition to understanding what academic requirements you need to fulfill for certification from the college, you should spend some time determining what the high school expects from you while you are teaching there.

CASE STUDY: PREPARING FOR STUDENT TEACHING

Harold Bricker
Supervisor of Student Teachers
Penn State Harrisburg
Middletown, PA
butchbricker@comcast.net

Harold "Butch" Bricker is currently the Supervisor of Student Teaching at Penn State-Harrisburg. He holds a bachelor's and a master's degree in social sciences. He has worked in the field of education for 40 years. Prior to working with student teachers at Penn State Harrisburg, he taught social studies at Camp Hill and Cumberland Valley High Schools; and served as an assistant principal, principal, director of secondary education, and assistant superintendent at Cumberland Valley High School. Here is his list of tips for anyone preparing for their student teacher internship.

- **Have clearances ready.** Before student teaching begins, make sure you have a TB test and all your clearances in order so you meet the requirements to student teach.
- **Contact cooperating teacher.** As soon as you receive your student teaching assignment, contact your cooperating teacher to see when you can meet with them. Arrange a meeting at his or her convenience so you can discuss your teaching assignment.
- **Understand the assignment.** Familiarize yourself with the lessons you will be teaching. Request a copy of the textbook and other materials that might help you prepare.
- **Make a good first impression.** When you meet, it is extremely important that you make a good first impression. Dress professionally. If you have piercings, take them out. If you have tattoos, keep them covered. Be very polite, enthusiastic, and always respectful.
- **Ask questions.** Ask meaningful question to help you understand what you will be doing, but don't ask needless questions or try to dominate conversations.

- **Learn about the school.** As soon as you receive your teaching assignment, visit the school district's Web site. Learn as much about the school and community as possible.
- **Know who is in charge.** Learn the names of key figures in the administration.
- **Know the school policies.** If the student handbook is on line, read it thoroughly. If not, ask for a copy.
- **Use your handbook.** Become familiar with your college student teaching handbook and all the requirements associated with student teaching. If you get an early start on all the above, you will feel more prepared and comfortable as you begin your assignment.
- **Work when the teacher works.** Plan to be at school the same hours as your cooperating teacher.
- **Do not miss work.** Don't be absent unless you are very ill.
- **Student teaching is your priority this semester.** If you have a part-time job, you may want to consider not working during student teaching. A teacher's day can be challenging and exhausting. Additionally, you will need a large amount of time in the evenings to prepare your lessons. This is the beginning of great opportunity to see what teaching is really like.
- **Make the most out of the experience.** Work hard, ask for feedback on a regular basis from your co-op and college supervisor, and have fun.
- **Have realistic expectations.** Understand that you will have some good days and some bad days.
- **Reevaluate and decide.** When your student teaching assignment is over, you will know whether this is the right profession for you.

Substitute teaching

Some individuals are lucky enough to be offered a job while they are doing their student teaching in their last semester of college. Most people, however, have to spend time looking for a job after they graduate, or at another point in their life. This is a good time to accrue other teaching experience until you get a full-time job. One of the best ways to do this is through substitute teaching. Whether you went to school to become a teacher and do not have a job yet or you are thinking about entering the profession as a second career, substitute teaching is a great way to get experience in the field.

A substitute teacher is one who stands in for the regular teacher when he or she is unable to be in the classroom for the day or even part of a day. Each district maintains a substitute list. This is a list of individuals that may be called upon to fill in for regular teachers, either for scheduled absences or short notice emergency reasons. Although each school district has its own regulations for substitute teachers, most schools do not require substitute teachers to have a degree in education. Check with your school district to see what the qualifications are for getting on the substitute list at the local high schools.

All school districts keep a substitute list. The list contains eligible individuals and their credentials. To get on the district's sub list, you will at least need the following:

- Résumé or curriculum vitae
- Copy of teaching certificate and licensure (where required)
- Completed application
- Necessary clearance documentation

Once you submit your application to the district office, if it is a public school then the school board reviews it. In cases of private or other school types, it may only need to be reviewed by a principal or other administrator. Once you receive approval, you are placed on a list and a substitute coordinator can call you at any time.

CASE STUDY: CALLING ALL SUBSTITUTES

Vicky Weidner
Human Resources Coordinator
Cumberland Valley School District
Mechanicsburg, PA
www.cvschools.org

Cumberland Valley School District uses several types of substitutes: professionals, nurses, support staff, guest teachers, and retirees. Professional substitutes must have a teaching certificate and nurse substitutes must have a nursing certificate. Guest Teachers must have a college degree but not a teaching certificate.

In order to become a substitute teacher in the district, individuals must acquire an information packet. It can be picked up in the district office or online at **www.cvschools.org**. In addition to filling out the packet, applicants must submit a résumé, pass a TB test, and have all the necessary clearances required for working with children in Pennsylvania. Please note that all clearances must be less than one year old to be considered applicable. These include:

- Act 34 Clearance (PA Criminal Background Check)
- Act 151 Clearance (Child Abuse Clearance)
- Act 114 Clearance (FBI Fingerprinting Criminal Background Check)

All of the district's substitutes must be Board-approved; however, once the necessary paperwork is completed, the district can place substitutes on the call list pending Board approval. Cumberland Valley uses the state-mandated guidelines for Pennsylvania professional substitutes, based on the Pennsylvania State Education Retirement System (PSERS) guidelines. Substitutes must be called in the following order:

- Professional substitutes
- Guest teachers
- Retirees

In other words, if an absence is scheduled, the district must first attempt to fill the position with a professional certified substitute. If none are available, the spot may be filled with a guest teacher substitute. Lastly, if neither are available, a retiree may be used. According to Pennsylvania state law, retired teachers may not be called unless all other options are exhausted first. Violations to this policy may affect retirement pension plans. Exceptions to this rule only apply in cases of emergency, such as last-minute call-offs.

Cumberland Valley School District uses an automated system called Aesop to notify substitutes of vacancies. Employees enter their absences into Aesop. Once the absence is entered, a substitute can log on to Aesop and view available jobs, choosing the positions in which they are interested. If the position is not filled within the two days prior to the absence, Aesop will phone all available substitutes. The fill rate with Aesop is much higher than the district's previous use of a substitute coordinator because Aesop allows substitutes to be proactive and responsible for their own schedules. Aesop follows the PSERS guidelines, offering positions to substitutes in the appropriate manner as explained above.

In the last ten years, there has been a shortage of teachers and substitute teachers. To compensate, many states created programs to prepare individuals to work in the classroom. These courses are called "guest teacher programs." These are for individuals who do not have education degrees, but wish to work in the teaching profession on a part-time basis. Most schools require substitutes to have an undergraduate Bachelor's degree and at least some training to prepare them for the classroom. If you did not go to college specifically to become a teacher, but are thinking of entering the profession, this is an opportunity for you to see if you would like to work in a secondary school; this is an excellent opportunity for determining whether it is a good match for you.

Each state has its own requirements for becoming a substitute teacher. To obtain your state's requirements for substitute teaching, check the Internet. One source for this information is the Become a Substitute Teacher Web site at **www.teacher-world.com/substitute-teacher.html**. By substituting, you gain experience and build relationships — this may help you if jobs open up in that school in the future. If not, you may at least be able to increase your pool of references.

There are many opportunities for teaching. If you are not currently employed full-time in the field, there are multiple ways to gain experience and build your résumé. For example:

- Acting as a teacher's assistant or aide
- Tutoring
- Providing lessons
- Coaching
- Mentoring
- Volunteering in a youth-centered activity, such as a church youth group

CASE STUDY: GAINING EXPERIENCE IN SUPPORT STAFF POSITIONS

Deborah Jones
Permanent Substitute
Chambersburg Area School District
Chambersburg, PA

Deb Jones is a permanent substitute for Chambersburg Area School District. For medical reasons, she chose the flexibility of substituting over accepting a permanent position. By agreeing to substitute in support staff positions, she increased the amount of job assignments available to her. She believes she has benefited greatly by gaining experience in a number of different positions in multiple schools.

Substituting in staff support positions offers many different types of experiences that can be useful in the teaching profession. It also offers you a new perspective on the other jobs in the school, and ultimately provides you with a better understanding and appreciation for everyone's part in getting things to run smoothly.

I have substituted for secretaries, personal aids, classroom aids, and lunchroom aids. I have enjoyed the variety and the chance to see many different schools in the district as well as working with children at all grade levels. There are positions available on a daily basis, so I am able to work any day that school is in session.

When I am called for a job, I may only be given the title and place I need to be. More specific instructions are provided when I get to the school in question. By being open to the possibilities, I am constantly gaining new job skills and gathering additional experience. Each position brings new challenges and a feeling of accomplishment. I have been lucky enough to substitute in a multitude of positions in the district, learning something new from each endeavor.

As a personal aid, I work one-on-one helping individual students who need a little more direction and attention. I help keep them on task, and assist them with getting homework completed. Working with the students makes me feel important, needed, and gives me a sense of accomplishment after each day. The students respond well to the one-on-one attention.

As classroom aid, I work in a specific classroom all day helping the teacher with a variety of items such as bulletin boards, copying, laminating, sorting, grading, and getting projects ready for the students.

I have also substituted for office personnel. As a secretary, I have used interpersonal skills to answer calls from parents. I have had to employ excellent organizational skills while filing, copying, and aiding teachers with numerous tasks that need to be done every day.

I have even worked as a cafeteria aid, teaching me how to keep order and discipline in a large group of children. I love my job and I believe it is important and valuable. If I were to give advice to anyone planning on working in a school environment, I would say this:

- You need to love children and want to make a difference.
- Never take anyone for granted.
- Pay attention to the tasks being done by others. Everyone matters.
- Love what you do.

Chapter 2

Location, Location, Location

"A teacher affects eternity; he can never tell where his influence stops."

— Henry Brooks Adams, American novelist (1838-1918)

Deciding What Environment to Work In

There are many factors you need to consider before choosing an environment to work in. Here are some points to consider:

- What area of the country do you want to work in?
- How far are you willing to travel to go to work each day?
- Is income a predominant deciding factor?
- Do you prefer an urban, suburban, or rural setting?
- Do you prefer to teach to a small group or a larger class?
- Would you prefer teaching in a public school, a private school, or another alternative, such as a charter school?
- How important is working in an environment with endless resources and the most current technological advances?

It is important to be honest with yourself as you answer these questions. Many people are impetuous when they take their first job, settling for whatever is offered to them. Resist the temptation to just take any job. Better yet, be sure to apply only to schools you feel will be a good match. For example, if you grew up in the city and thrive on a fast-paced environment, a rural setting may not be the right choice for you. The following is information on various types of secondary school environments.

Area of the county

- **Urban**: The United States Census Bureau defines an urban area as one that has a population density of at least 1,000 people per square mile.

- **Suburban**: In the United States, suburban areas are characterized by small plots of land, single-family homes, and a higher standard of living. Suburban areas have a prevalence of usually detached single-family homes. Urban and suburban areas contain 75 percent of all individuals living the U.S.

- **Rural**: The Census Bureau found that rural areas comprise 98 percent of the land in the United States even though they have the lowest population density. An area can be considered rural with a population density between 1 and 999 people per square mile.

Size of school

- **Large**: Secondary schools in the country with an excess of 500 students per grade.
- **Small**: Secondary schools with less than 100 students per grade.

Type of school

- **Public**: A U.S. school that does not require tuition from the students. It is funded by taxes and run by a school board.

- **Private (for profit)**: Privately established schools that are run without government assistance and are supported by endowment and tuition. For-profit institutions are businesses that charge more and make money in the process.

- **Charter schools**: Experimental schools created and organized by teachers and parents and community leaders. They are run like businesses and operate independently of other schools. They receive public money but are free from many of the public school regulations. In exchange for the funds, they have some degree of accountability for producing certain results, set forth in each school's charter.

- **Private, parochial, or other non-profit**: Schools open to a select number of individuals who fit certain criteria and/or pay tuition. Religious schools fall into this category.

Area of the country and how it affects education

There are numerous job opportunities for teachers all over the world. This book, however, concentrates on careers in the United States. That being said, the United States is huge. According to the last census, there were 53.3 million children between the ages 5 to 17 living in 50 different states, in countless different environments. Additionally, the way the United States handles education and funding is constantly changing. There are still a large number of children in this country who are not getting a good education. State testing requirements are in place to help identify schools that are under-performing. Schools that fall in this spectrum have three years to make adjustments and improve student scores. If a school is unable to comply, the government may come in and make massive changes. These changes include dismissing administrators and teachers, and in some cases, disbanding the school entirely. It is important for you to understand how your school fairs in respect to meeting the state requirements, because it could ultimately affect your job. If the school fails to meet its goals, it may be eligible for grant money to help make the necessary improvements, but these improvements may include the elimination of current staff.

On Dec. 3, 2009, U.S. Secretary of Education Arne Duncan announced plans for allocating $3.5 billion to low-performing schools that meet the requirements of the Title I School Improvement grant project. The grant money is available to school districts that apply, meet the criteria, and are willing to adhere to one of the following four transformation models:

1. **Turnaround model:** In the turnaround model, the school needs to be willing to agree to major changes. First, the district must be willing to replace the existing principal. Additionally, the staff must undergo a major overhaul, with no more than 50 percent of the former staff retaining their positions. The new principal must be granted a certain amount of flexibility as it pertains to staffing, time allocation, and budgeting in the approach to improve the school and the student outcomes.

2. **Restart model:** In the restart model, the school in question must consent to close and reopen in a different manner, such as a charter school operator, a charter management organization, or an education management organization. To be eligible, the school must submit to an arduous review process.

3. **School closure:** In some cases, the school must be permanently closed In these instances, the students from the school in question are disbanded and re-enrolled in another school in the same area that has better student outcomes.

4. **Transformation model:** In the transformation model, schools must implement specific strategies. They must include all of the following:

- Replace the principal
- Take initiative in improving school leader and teacher effectiveness
- Be willing to institute comprehensive instructional reforms
- Increase amount of learning time

- Create community-oriented schools
- Provide operational flexibility and sustained support

Student outcomes are not the only factor to consider when looking at schools. There are a number of environmental issues to consider as well. Schools are classified in many ways. To simplify the categories, school types are broken down into three primary groupings: urban, suburban, and rural schools. This does not mean that every school in this country falls directly into one of these categories, but it may help you ascertain a general region you prefer working and living in. Some of the general pros and cons of each type of school are listed below.

Urban schools

What should you expect if you take a job in an urban or inner-city high school? Let us look at the pros and cons:

Pros:

- Potentially higher salaries.
- Signing bonuses to attract new teachers.
- Cultural diversity.
- Some schools in these areas will entice new teachers by offering to pay off student loans.
- The need for good teachers in these areas is important.
- Provides a challenge and an increased sense of accomplishment when success is achieved
- Assistance available from programs, such as: The Center for Urban School Partnerships at Texas A&M University. Visit the Web site at **http://tlac.tamu.edu**. The CUSP center researches and offers support to projects on collaborative learning in urban education environments. One of these CUSP initiatives offers mentoring veteran teachers through professional development for urban teaching. Another program is the Urban Teacher Enhancement

Program (UTEP), through the University of Alabama. Their Web site is located at **www.ed.uab.edu/utep** and offers urban school recruitment, tuition support, and mentoring for new teachers, among other resources.

Cons:

- Lack of funding stemming from impoverished areas.
- Lack of resources because of diminished funds.
- Outdated textbooks and other materials, potentially creating problems with the curriculum.
- Overcrowded classrooms and potentially rundown facilities.
- Students with significant problems outside of school.
- High student turnover and an increased dropout rate.
- Apathetic students creating an overall lower achievement level.
- Potential for insecurity, fear, fatigue, and stress are greater for new teachers, particularly if they are unfamiliar with the environment.

Suburban schools

What should you expect if you take a job in a suburban high school? Let us look at the pros and cons:

Pros:

- Average to above average income areas result in greater taxes and increased funds.
- Increased funding provides for better supplies, materials, and field trips.
- Better overall resources that are less likely to be outdated.

- Lower dropout rate.
- Greater overall achievement rate, which some studies suggest is directly proportionate to the income levels of the surrounding area.
- Increased security to combat challenges.

Cons:

- Increased family income may cause entitlement and apathy among students.
- Potential for decreased cultural diversity, depending on area.
- Not a significantly challenging environment.
- More desirable neighborhoods create greater competition for jobs.
- Larger pool of applicants may lead to lower salaries and benefits.

Rural schools

What should you expect if you take a job in a rural high school? Let us look at the pros and cons:

Pros:

- Generally smaller class size.
- Less competition for jobs.
- Slower lifestyle pace for those who prefer this lifestyle.
- Potentially safer environment.
- Supplemental income and resources from programs such as Rural Education Achievement Program (REAP).

Cons:

- Limited district funds translate into decreased curriculum offerings.
- Potential for decreased cultural diversity, depending on area.

- Poverty is usually an issue.
- Distance between locations is generally farther, equating to a potentially farther commute.
- Potentially outdated resources and materials.
- Less technology for educational purposes.
- Decreased program options.
- Higher dropout rates at the high school level when individuals begin working to take over the family business.
- Confusion and despair in areas where farmland is being sold and developed.
- Lower self-esteem and lower achievement rates among students.
- Lower salaries.
- Fewer available jobs.
- Increased responsibilities for teachers.

The issue of size

How does the size of a school affect its teachers? Does it have a general impact on salaries and curriculum? Thoughts concerning school size continue to change. In the 1950s, studies suggested the need for larger schools. The belief was that schools with enrollments in excess of 1,000 students created greater competition and a better chance for producing the top minds. The experiment was to create more of these larger institutions to combat the issues of the Cold War. Since then, school size has been debated several times. At any given time, there have been arguments producing data on either side. Here are some of the prevailing thoughts on both sides of the debate. The bottom line is choosing the environment you feel most comfortable in.

Large high schools (1,000 or more students)

Pros:

- A larger pool of students, creating greater competition and higher achievement rates.
- Increased course offerings.
- Potential for increased resources, depending on location of the school and its budget.
- More people mean more chances for students to find a niche and find others like them to develop friendships with, creating less isolation issues for teachers.
- Increases chance of diversity.

Cons:

- Larger schools may mean less money spent per student.
- Less potential for direct teacher-student interaction.

Looking for a job is a numbers game. Once you decide what type of environment you want to work in, start researching jobs in that area. Information pertaining to school type and student teacher ratio is available online. There are Web sites that provide this information to assist parents looking for the right school for their children. It applies to teachers as well. These sites provide detailed demographic information about high schools in the United States:

- **GreatSchools**: A national nonprofit that contains profiles and reviews for each school, and allows you to browse schools by city (**www.greatschools.net/high-school/**)
- **High-Schools.com**: Provides statistical data on public and private U.S. high school based on information provided by the National Center for Education Statistics (**http://high-schools.com**)
- **Local Schools Directory**: Provides data (broken down by national, state, and local) on K-12, such as statistics, mailing lists, reviews, and events (**www.localschooldirectory.com**)

If you prefer a larger school district, the following are the top ten largest school districts in the United States. This information was compiled in 2009 and appeared on the Local School Directory Web site. For the most current information, check the Web site at **www.localschooldirectory.com**. Under the "National Statistics" section, you can find information on districts nationwide.

TOP TEN U.S. SCHOOL DISTRICTS			
Rank	*School District*	*Total Number of Schools*	*Total Enrollment*
1	Los Angeles Unified School District	811	702,763
2	City of Chicago School District 299	652	412,294
3	Dade County School District	399	349,531
4	Clark School District	318	293,008
5	Houston Independent School District	318	202,872
6	Broward County School District	286	261,823
7	Hawaii Department of Education School District	285	180,289
8	Philadelphia City School District	278	174,236
9	Hillsborough County School District	265	191,235
10	Detroit City School District	262	117,221

Small high schools (500 or less total students)

Pros:

- Smaller class size (one private school in New York only has four high school students).
- Lower student-teacher ratio.
- Increased awareness of student's individual circumstances.
- Potential for increased family involvement, depending on school type.
- Potential for increased earnings, depending on school type.

Cons:

- Less privacy — because of the smaller size, everyone tends to know everything about everyone else.

- Potential for lower wages, depending on school type. Teachers at small parochial schools tend to make the least amount of money.
- Decreased chance of diversity.
- Less potential for competition.
- Greater potential for isolation issues among fringe students.

The debate continues on the advantages and disadvantages of school size. The opinion changes each year. Current documentation tends to be in favor of small schools, in respect to student success. However, they have the highest turnover rate amongst faculty.

The smallest high schools in the country tend to be private institutions. If you want to work with fewer students, you may want to research these types of schools. There are different types of private schools as well. There are schools that make a profit and may pay more, and there are non-profit private schools, such as parochial and other religious institutions. Please visit the "Smallest Enrollment" section of the 2010 U.S. News & World Report, "America's Best High Schools," for a list of top-ranked schools with enrollment ranging from 47 to 150: **www.usnews.com/sections/education/high-schools**.

Different types of schools offer different environments

Public schools: This is the most prevalent form of education in the United States. Approximately 88 percent of all school-aged students in the U.S. attend public schools. These institutions are those that do not require students to pay tuition. The government funds the schools with income derived primarily from local property taxes. Decisions concerning finances, curriculum, policy issues, and teachers are made by a locally elected group of individuals known as a school board. Each school district, an area designated by the state, has its own school board. For more information on the public schools in your area, refer to the following Public School Review Web site**: www.publicschoolreview.com**.

Pros:

- Increased chance of diversity
- Possibility for increased earning potential
- Government funding may allow for better resources, depending on school location
- Additional programs in the arts may exist
- Assistance provided for special needs students

Cons:

- Government mandates may hinder teachers' freedom in curriculum
- Depending on school location, funding may result in less resources
- Direct correlation between socio-economic factors and student achievement
- Increased potential for challenges with disruptive students
- Significant emphasis on state testing

Charter schools: The first charter school started in St. Paul, Minnesota, in 1992. Since then, they have become increasingly popular. A charter school is a specific type of public school that operates without many of the regulations affecting traditional public schools. These alternative schools still must provide 180 days of instruction and must take part in state testing, but are exempt from numerous other government mandated school policies, as stated in the state's charter laws. For example, according to their charter, these are a few of the items Pennsylvania Charter schools are exempt from:

- Driver education course standards
- 25-pupil class size limit
- Requirements to maintain grades kindergarten through twelfth
- Latchkey operating requirements

These schools have a document, or charter, that serves as a performance contract. It explains the school's directives. They include the charter school's mission statement as well as information concerning the programs and proposed student outcomes. There are additional specifics related to the methods of assessment. Most charter schools are granted their status for approximately three to five years. At the conclusion of the charter, the school must provide documentation on the results to their sponsor, which is generally the school board. At that time, they may apply to renew their charter. The documentation pertains to a statement of accountability agreed upon at the time of the original charter. Each charter contains goals unique to the individual school. They concern student achievement and operational functions. The charters contain mission statements and concise measurable goals.

For example, according to the New York State Education Department, the Data-driven Differentiated Instruction and Learning Project (D3IL) is a partnership of ten separate New York City charter schools. The project began in 2007 under the direction of the Partnership for Innovation in Compensation for Charter Schools (PICCS). The **www.nysed.gov** Web site lists the goals of Williamsburg Charter High School as part of the D3IL partnership. The goals are:

1. Increase the leadership skills of participating building administrators to create professional learning communities of teachers that work to increase data literacy among all staff.

2. Design and implement school- and grade-level collaboration strategies that emphasize shared norms and values, ongoing data-driven dialogue and collaborative inquiry, with sufficient time and structure for collaboration.

3. Increase the type, amount, and frequency of data used by the entire school community as part of the ongoing system for continuous improvement to enhance instructional practice and increase student learning.

4. Improve instructional skills of teachers as measured by the alignment of learning goals, instruction, and assessments, the utiliza-

tion of research and best practices, and supplemental programs and interventions to prevent failure.

5. Create a culture that supports internal responsibility rather than external accountability and focuses on opportunities for all.

6. Add to teachers' professional belief systems that all children are capable of high levels of achievement.

For a charter school to be able to stay open and renew their charter, they must be able to prove with documented measurable statistics, that they have met each of the goals stated in the charter.

According to the U.S. Charter Schools Web site (**www.uscharterschools.org**), these schools are preferable because although they receive some public funding, they are independent from government intervention. Instead, they have an increased accountability to the charter's sponsor. They must be accountable fiscally and academically to the charter sponsor, the community that funds them, the students, and the parents who choose to send their children there. According to the most current documentation, more than 1.2 million students are currently enrolled in charter schools in the United States.

A recent study shows increased performance from the charter high schools. The study was conducted by the Research and Development Corporation (RAND), in conjunction with Mathematical Policy Research, Inc., and two colleges: Florida State University and Michigan State University. The RAND results depicted students attending charter high school to be "7 to 15 percentage points more likely to earn a standard diploma than students who attend a traditional public high school" the study also stated that charter high school students are "8 to 10 percentage points more likely to attend college" than their public school counterparts.

President Obama is currently focused on improving the United States School System. A recent report from the Alliance for Excellent Education stated that currently only 71 percent of high school students in the United States graduate with a regular diploma in four years. Given these statistics, the trend in the near future may be to increase the number of charter schools. So charter school teaching jobs could continue to increase in number in the years to come.

Pros:

- Exemption from government regulations provides more freedom.
- Increased earning potential for teachers, depending on school. (Note: A new charter school in New York offered a salary of $125,000 in order to obtain the best teachers.)
- Lower student-teacher ratio.
- Smaller class size.
- Safer environment.
- Greater chance for one-on-one instruction to meet individual needs.
- Higher academic standards.
- Increased availability of quality educational resources.
- Teacher freedom allowing increased chance for creativity.
- Increased parental involvement.
- Potential for higher wages.

Cons:

- Schools operate as businesses, and may be affected by economic fluctuations.
- Decreased job stability.
- Increased potential for challenges in accountability.
- Student performance is difficult to measure and enforce.
- Less chance for diversity and socialization.
- Decreased support for special needs.

Private schools: According to the Council for American Private Education (CAPE), 11 percent of all students in kindergarten through twelfth grade were registered to attend private schools during the beginning of the 2009 school term. In the United States, private schools are independent entities not funded and therefore not directly run by the government. As a result, these schools are able to select and retain students of their choice. Most private schools are funded entirely, or at least partially, by student tuition. There are several categories of private schools:

1. **Preparatory ("prep") schools.** Prep schools can be boarding schools or the day school variety. They offer to prepare students for college. They are unique in their ability to charge increased tuitions in order to make a profit. In return, they maintain higher standards and offer the best facilities and materials, better teachers, and lower student-to-teacher ratios. Many of these schools are privately owned and operated. Since the majority of private schools do not accept public funding, they are not bound by federal and state mandates. In other words, they are not affected by the No Child Left Behind laws, and therefore teachers do not need to "teach to the test."

Pros:

- In boarding schools, teacher housing is often provided, offsetting cost-of-living expenses.
- Higher potential for increased earnings than parochial counterparts.
- Smaller class size.
- Lower student-teacher ratios.
- Increased family incomes may result in better resources for the school.
- Studies have shown a potential for greater academic competition and higher achievement rates at many of these schools.
- School uniforms decrease dress code problems.
- Teachers do not need to plan lesson plans around mandated tests.

Cons:

- Potential for less diversity, potentially in the socio-economic category.

- Possibility of entitlement issues among parents and students.

2. **Military academies.** A military high school is a school that places value on tradition, discipline and honor. The schools have traditional high school subjects, but also encourage physical and military training. Unlike military schools in some other countries, the United States military schools are all privately owned and operated. They have never received public funds. During the early 1800s, the Continental Congress debated developing these types of schools, but decided against it. They agreed only to provide funds for a military college instead. As a result, the United States Military Academy at West Point was developed. West Point opened in 1802 during Thomas Jefferson's presidency. At this time, military schools were very popular in the United States. Some of them are still in operation today. For example, St. John's Military School in Kansas was founded in 1887 and was awarded the Parent's Top Choice Private School Award in 2009.

Pros:

- Long-standing traditions.
- Excellent academics.
- Military training for those individuals who plan on careers as military officers..
- Higher pay than public schools.
- Sense of teamwork.
- Honor and ethics valued.
- Discipline in enforced.
- Uniforms eliminate dress-code issues.

Cons:

- Many military schools are known for being private reform schools for troubled teenagers.
- Requires military training.
- Not for those who thrive on creativity and open expression.

3. **Religious schools.** Another subcategory of private schools includes those that are religiously affiliated. Many of these schools, such as Catholic schools, include religious education as part of the curriculum. Other religious schools are merely labeled to denote the beliefs of the school's founders. There are multiple denominations providing specific schools in the United States. The following, according the National Center of Education Statistics (NCES), is a chart depicting a breakdown of religious private schools during the 2007-2008 school year for K-12:

Orientation	Percentage Distribution of Private Schools
Roman Catholic	22.2
Amish	3.1
Assembly of God	1.2
Baptist	6.8
Brethren	0.2
Calvanist	0.4
Christian (unspecified)	13.8
Church of Christ	0.7
Church of God	0.4
Church of God in Christ	0.1
Church of the Nazarene	0.2
Episcopal	1.2
Friends	0.3
Greek Orthodox	0.1
Islamic	0.7
Jewish	3.0
Lutheran Church — Missouri Synod	3.6
Evangelical Lutheran Church in America	0.5
Wisconsin Evangelical Lutheran Synod	1.0
Other Lutheran	0.2
Mennonite	1.3
Methodist	0.9
Pentecostal	1.1
Presbyterian	1.1

Seventh-Day Adventist	2.5
Other	1.3
Nonsectarian	31.2

Since a majority of private and religious schools in the country are Catholic, specific information concerning those schools is included here. According to the National Catholic Education Association, there were 7,094 Catholic schools operating in the United States during the 2009 to 2010 school term. Those schools include enrollments of more than two million students and have waiting lists for more than 1,700 students. These schools employ 154.316 professional staff members — approximately 4 percent of that number are religious personnel.

Catholic schools in the United States are accredited by independent and/or state agencies. The schools are primarily supported through tuition payments but subsidize their expenses through the church and fund raising. There are scholarships and vouchers funded by the private sector and the government to allow admittance to those who are financially challenged. Some Catholic schools have their own school board with the parish priest as a member of the board, while others are run by the diocese with the bishop acting in the role of superintendent.

There has been a decline in the amount of these types of schools over the last decade. They are still favored, however, in many inner city areas. In fact, over 42 percent of the Catholic schools in the U.S. today are located in urban areas. For more specific information concerning Catholic schools, refer to the National Catholic Education Association Web site at **www.ncea.org**.

Pros:

- Smaller school environment
- Smaller class size
- Lower student-to-teacher ratio
- Stricter rules provide more teacher control
- Greater potential for family involvement

- Uniforms lessen dress code issues; teachers do not need to deal with students dressed inappropriately
- More curriculum control for administrators and teachers, because mandated tests do not apply
- Ability for school to remove disruptive students

Cons:

- Lower salaries
- In times of economic challenges, lower enrollment may force teacher layoffs or school closings
- Less chance of diversity, particularly by exposure to alternate religious views
- Decreased course selections
- Decreased chance of teachers receiving assistance for special needs students
- Need to teach religion as part of the curriculum (a negative if you do not fully embrace the views)

4. **Special assistance schools.** In addition to the schools mentioned above, there are approximately 90 schools in the United States devoted specifically to providing an education to students with special needs. Many students who need special attention are attending main stream schools, but some parents feel that their children need a different type of environment with teachers trained to work with individuals with special needs. These schools offer that assistance.

Pros:

- Small student-to-teacher ratio.
- Environment tailored to special needs kids and equipped with all necessary materials.
- High salary potential in this private school atmosphere than in similar job at public school.

- Less conflicts arising from interactions between individuals insensitive to special needs.

Cons:

- Less diversity.
- Challenging, sometimes depressing environment.
- Usually, you must complete extra schooling or certification in order to work at these institutions. This may not be possible for some.

5. **Cyber schools.** Another type of school system has emerged recently. It is online education. Online schools, or cyber schools, provide an alternative to traditional forms of education. In many instances, traditional schooling is not working for these students. Cyber schools allow individuals the ability to obtain a home-schooled education from a teacher other than their parents. The courses are offered through the use of a personal computer. All different types of schools offer this type of education, including public, charter, and private schools. It is another opportunity to research when looking for teaching jobs.

   Cyber education is still a relatively new concept. Some are funded by the state, while others are privately owned and operated. If this is something you are interested in pursuing, you may find information at the Online High Schools Web site at **www.cyber-highschools.com**.

Pros:

- Virtual teaching jobs allow you flexibility in working wherever you want.
- Some opportunities offer flexibility in hours.
- Small class size.
- Multiple opportunities to teach different subjects.

- Many job opportunities to teach English as a second language to other countries.
- Depending on the program, you may not require an education degree.

Cons:

- Not a traditional classroom environment.
- Lower paying jobs than most public schools.
- May be frustrating for those who prefer a more hands-on approach to teaching.

"I currently teach geography to approximately 100 students enrolled in the PA Cyber School. One of the biggest advantages is the ability to keep teaching without disruptions. This kind of environment makes classroom management relatively easy, by eliminating most behavioral issues."

— Jim VanderSchaaff, social studies teacher, PA Cyber School

Before you begin the application process, take time to review the factors that are most important to you. Research sources online to find out which school districts meet your needs. Again, the National Center for Education Statistics Web site includes information about each district in the country at **www.nces.ed.gov**. From there, you can determine the types of schools in each district. With modern technology, virtually all the information you need is available online. If you prefer looking through a book, *Patterson's American Education,* a reference book compiled and published by Educational Directories, lists facts pertaining to each school district in every state. The book is updated each October.

CASE STUDY: WHY I LOVE TEACHING AT A PAROCHIAL SCHOOL

John Cominsky
Religion Teacher
Trinity High School
Mechanicsburg, PA
jcomins@trinityhs.k12.pa.us

John Cominsky has taught religion at Trinity High School in Mechanicsburg, Pennsylvania, since 1994. Currently, he teaches religion to sophomores and juniors. Sophomore religion covers scripture studies, and junior-year religion covers ethics and moral issues. For the past five years, Cominsky also served as an adjunct professor at Mount St. Mary's University in Emmitsburg, Maryland, teaching two core requirement courses: Foundations of Theology and Gospels. In addition to teaching at the high school and college level, he is currently pursuing his second master's degree. In his case study, he explains his reasons for preferring the Catholic school environment.

I am in my sixteenth year of teaching Catholic education. My college major was theology, so teaching in a Catholic school was a simple choice, and I graduated from Trinity High School. Coming back to my alma mater was a natural decision as well. Since I went to Catholic schools and have taught in Catholic schools, that is what I know best. Here are my thoughts on why I prefer the Catholic school environment:

1. Catholic school teachers may address the development of the whole person. This includes the ability to offer religious education, retreats, moral instruction, liturgies, and other related endeavors. In my own case, I teach sophomore and junior-year religion classes. In the moral issues course, we discuss topics such as the death penalty, abortion, euthanasia, and poverty. I cannot imagine offering such a class in an area public school district.

2. Catholic schools require mandatory service hours. We have a mandatory service program that is evaluated by the religion department. It requires each student to offer 20 service hours of volunteer time per year to approved charities and individuals. The program is based on the Corporal Works of Mercy from Matthew 25. Many of

our kids do the same project for extended periods of time — even after high school — building a relationship with a charity or cause.

3. Catholic schools require parent involvement. Parents are asked to volunteer their time and talents to help the school function properly. While many teachers may see parents as interfering from time to time, ultimately I believe that our parents are more "in touch" with the happenings of the school because they are directly responsible for many events.
4. Catholic schools are far more independent, in my opinion, than public schools. This pertains to curriculum, extracurricular activities, and sports. I suppose this can be viewed as a positive and a negative, but in my experience it has been a positive.
5. Catholic schools can remove students when needed. Although public districts may also do so, Catholic schools have a different set of expectations. The tolerance level is low for students who do not want to be there and do not act appropriately. I spend very little time with "classroom management" because of the expectations that our school has regarding its learning environment.
6. Catholic schools are far less susceptible to political "whims" or changes that accompany the election of a new board by the populace. In particular, I am thinking of the Dover School Board (in Dover, Pennsylvania). The school attempted to institute creationism into the science classes, only to be voted out after becoming the subject of national attention and media debate.
7. Unions are not as big of a focus at religious schools than at many public schools. Some Catholic schools have unions, but they do not exist here in the Diocese of Harrisburg. I go back and forth on this issue myself. Unions provide teachers with protection and benefits, but they also have downsides. I believe there is far less of an adversarial relationship between faculty and administration in Catholic schools that do not have unions. Of course, this depends on the administrator. Ironically, everyone knows the salaries here will lag behind (our salaries are only about 70 percent of those teaching in this area's public schools). Knowing that ahead of time actually makes it less of an issue for many of our teachers.

Chapter 3

In Pursuit of a Job

"Teaching should be such that what is offered is perceived as a valuable gift and not as a hard duty."

— Albert Einstein, theoretical physicist (1879-1955)

After acquiring the necessary accreditation and working in the high school environment, you have decided that you really enjoy teenagers and you want to obtain a permanent position. What do you need to do next? First, you need to prepare your résumé. Then you need to look for a job, and finally, you need to prepare for the interview.

Introducing Yourself on Paper

When you decide the type of school you want to work in, you can begin the application process. Research schools that interest you and develop your résumé to highlight skills pertaining to the specific job you are seeking. Unless you are applying at the school where you did your student teaching, the application packet will be the school's first impression of you. For that reason, it is extremely important to get it right. There are four main parts to the written part of the application process. They are:

1. **Application** — A pre-printed form that must be filled out. Some states are working toward simplifying the application process.

They belong to an organization known as the National School Applications Network (NSAN). Schools belonging to this group have general forms online that may be downloaded and completed as part of the application process. As of March 2010, the following states participate with the NASN:

- Connecticut
- Iowa
- Kentucky
- Michigan
- Missouri
- New Mexico
- Ohio
- Pennsylvania
- Texas

If you are applying to a school in a state that does not participate, you may obtain applications at the school district office, online at the school district's Web site, or from the state Board of Education. Standard applications require the following:

- Position desired
- Name, address, e-mail address, phone number(s)
- Certification information, including area of certification, issuing state, and date issued
- Tenure status
- Date available for employment
- Education background
- Work experience
- Student or practice teaching information
- References
- Criminal activity questions
- Clearance/background check information
- Signature

In most cases, schools will require you to fill in the application even if you have a résumé or curriculum vitae attached. Some applications will also require you to write a personal statement or answer another essay question.

2. **Cover letter** — A letter that introduces yourself, explaining why you are seeking a certain position and why you are the person most suited for the job. The cover letter should be placed on top of the other papers in the front of the application packet. The letter should include a strong statement that will make the reader want to look at your application more closely.

3. **Résumé or curriculum vitae** — The formal documentation depicting your education, skills, and experience. This document also needs to stand out from others by highlighting the most important facts about you and your experience. A curriculum vitae (CV) may be a little longer but is not much different from a résumé. Even if you fill out an application with all of the necessary information concerning your education and experience, you should submit a formal résumé or CV with your application packet. It is much more professional.

4. **Follow-up letter** — The first three items are submitted together as an application packet. After you have submitted the packet, it is appropriate to write a follow-up letter in a few days to a week. The follow-up reintroduces you and helps you stand out from the other applicants. It does not need to be long. It should consist of the following elements:

    - *Greeting* — Simply restate who you are.
    - *Reason* — What position you are interested in.
    - *Attention grabber* — One or two specific relevant accomplishments that make you perfect for the job.

- *Request* — Statement requesting an interview, in other words: "I look forward to meeting with you to further discuss my qualifications."
- *Follow-up statement* — A note that states you expect to hear from them and will continue to follow-up if you do not. For example, "If I do not hear from you beforehand, I will follow-up with you in two weeks to set up a time to discuss my application."

5. **Thank you letter** — After you have met with a member of the human resources department or have been interviewed, you should send a thank you letter to the person you spoke with. This is another reminder of who you are. Sometimes, it is the follow-up letter or thank you note that makes the determination between two similar candidates.

Writing Your Résumé

Résumés often determine who gets to the interview stage. No matter how much experience you have or how great a teacher you are, you need to present yourself well on paper. In the field of education, there are two ways to display this information: a résumé or a CV. Regardless of which you choose, it is imperative that you make it look professional. Here are some tips for developing a professional document.

- **Use quality paper.** Use high-quality, 24-pound, watermarked paper. The extra cost of watermarked paper is worth the professionalism it reflects, and the added weight of the paper will ensure its sturdiness. Do not use anything with a bright color or a design on it. You want the words to stand out, not the paper.
- **Keep it simple.** It should be the neatly typed in a simple, easy-to-read font. Make it look professional. According to the Web site **www.resumes-for-teachers-.com**, the average résumé gets only

a cursory glance of ten to 20 seconds. The site also suggests that the document should be easy to read with bullet points and lots of white space.

- **Proofread.** If you are applying for a high school teaching position, you should not have any typographical or grammatical errors on your résumé. If you do, it is highly unlikely you will get the job. Once you have proofread it, give it to someone else to review as well, perhaps another teacher or an editor.

- **Add headings.** Bold headings will make the document easier to read. Add headings to identify specific areas of your information. For example, a high school teacher's résumé may include the following headings

    - *Objective* — Description of the job you desire, such as "enthusiastic educator seeking secondary school teaching position in positive environment."
    - *Experience* — List jobs and other teaching, training, and coaching experiences.
    - *Technical knowledge* — List skills that apply to the job, such as computer programs and knowledge of smart-boards.
    - *Education* — Colleges, degrees, workshops, and special training.
    - *Certification* — Information regarding your teaching certificate and license.
    - *References upon request*

- **Briefly describe education and employment experiences.** In addition to student teaching and substituting, do not forget to mention volunteer positions such as mentoring, tutoring, and coaching; any clubs or organizations you belong to; and any publications or projects you have worked on. Make sure they reflect the high school employee position you are seeking. If you are young and fresh out of college with limited work experience, think about the skills you have used even in your part-time employment and include them in your job description. For example, working in a fast food reference might not be a teaching job, but it is relevant. It provided you with a chance to improve your interpersonal and communication skills.

- **References upon request.** Type this statement at the bottom of your résumé. Type up a copy of your references and contact information and take it with you to the interview. Compile pertinent information concerning your references and have it readily available when asked for it. Of course, teaching references are optimal, but do not worry if this is your first professional employment search. Choose references who will tell a potential employer that you have a positive work ethic, which is a highly valued trait. Additionally, if you have worked on projects with your professors, ask them whether they will provide you with a reference. Showing you are a hardworking student speaks volumes for the type of example you will set for your own students.

If you have no idea where to start, do some research online. There are numerous Web sites that offer templates for résumés and cover letters. The following Web sites are three particularly helpful examples. They are specifically designed for assisting teachers in creating résumés and cover letters:

- Résumés for Teachers: **www.resumes-for-teachers.com/teacher-resume-examples.htm** — This Web site is geared specifically to teachers. It has numerous helpful suggestions on creating résumés and cover letters for any teaching job, and the site shows multiple examples. Additionally, the moderator Candace Davies provides contact information for anyone who has questions not already answered on the site.

- A to Z Teacher Stuff: **www.atozteacherstuff.com/pages/1876.shtml** — This Web site contains basic information on everything teachers need to know, including suggestions for effective résumés.

- Sample Résumés: **www.bestsampleresume.com/teachers-resumes.html** — has a couple of simple outline formats for prospective teachers to use as guidelines.

When creating your teacher's résumé, the following four areas are the most critical for showcasing who you are:

- **Identification**: All résumés should have your name in a large, bold clear font on the top. Under that, you should include your name, address, home and cell phone numbers, and your email address.

- **Career objective**: Include a statement about the type of job you are seeking. Include what type of environment you would prefer to work in.

- **Education and certification**: In addition to listing the schools you attended and the degrees you earned, you should provide any teaching certification you attained.

- **Teaching experience**: Be sure to highlight any actual teaching experience you may have. Include student teaching, substitute teaching, and any other related positions.

At the end of your document, you may add other pertinent information, such as professional development courses, special skills, achievements, and professional memberships. In addition to a flawless résumé, be sure to include a strong, well-written cover letter.

Do Not Forget the Cover Letter

Prospective employers usually expect personalized cover letters in addition to your résumé or curriculum vitae. Your cover letter is your opportunity to summarize your qualifications, highlight certain elements of your background, and convince employers to look at your résumé. It s not recommended you use a generic letter, as employers can usually spot them right away and it will count against you. Here are some other important points to consider:

- Limit your cover letter to one page.
- Address it to someone specific. Do the research and find out the name of the person doing the hiring. A letter addressed to "Dear Sir or Madam" is not very impressive.
- Briefly state the position you are interested in.
- Highlight just a few (not a huge list) of your strongest qualifications that make you perfect for the job.
- Mention something about the school that you like; a reason you may want to work there.
- State that you will follow-up with a call, and mention when. For example, "I will follow up with you next week to set up a time to meet and go over my application in person."
- Close with "Sincerely," and your name type written, as well as your signature.
- Add the word "enclosures" at the bottom to indicate that your résumé is included in the packet.

The Interview Process

If you have prepared an excellent application packet, you should hopefully be called for an interview. In order to obtain the job you want, you will first need to succeed in the interview. In order to do your best, prepare ahead of time. Research the school you apply to. Many of the interview questions may pertain to challenges specific to that school. Researching the school may also provide you with a list of questions to ask the interviewer. Displaying your knowledge of the school will impress the interviewer. In addition to knowing everything about the school, you need to prepare yourself. Be sure this is really what you want to do. If it is not, it will come across in your interview.

When preparing for your interview, keep in mind that the interview may take place with one person or multiple individuals. If this is the case, it will most likely be a principal, a superintendent, or human resources personnel. It is also possible that you will interview in front of a panel with as many as six people. Those six people may consist of the principal, the superintendent, and part of the school board. The following is a list of things to consider and review prior to attending the interview:

1. Review your résumé. Be sure you are able to answer any questions about your education, experience, and anything else on your résumé. The interviewer or interviewers will most likely have some questions about items on your résumé.

2. Understand your strengths and weaknesses. Be prepared to list them in the interview. How you answer these kinds of questions tells the interviewer a lot about you. For example, saying that your biggest weakness is your organization skills is not going to help you get the job. On the other hand, saying that your biggest weakness is a desire to go over your paperwork multiple times to ensure that you have not missed anything shows the interviewer that you are thorough.

3. Prepare possible answers to common interview questions prior to attending the interview. You do not need to write down the answers or memorize them, but you do need to be prepared for a variety of questions and scenarios. Many Web sites list potential interview questions online. Look for questions that are specific to teacher interviews. The following are a few sample interview questions to help you prepare:

- Why do you want to be teacher?

- What is your personal teaching philosophy?
- What appeals to you about working in a high school environment?
- Explain some of your recent experiences with teenagers.
- What aspect of teaching do you feel is the most rewarding?
- What aspect of teaching do you feel is the most challenging?
- Do you have experience working with special needs?
- What is your approach to classroom management and student discipline?
- Describe a particularly difficult circumstance you handled. What action did you take? What were the results?
- How would you handle a disruptive student in your class you believe to be under the influence of drugs or alcohol?
- Can you explain what professionalism means to you within the school climate and outside of school?
- As a high school teacher, what would you consider to be the worst scenario for you to deal with and how would you handle it?
- What are your personal and professional goals for this year?
- Where do you see yourself in five years?
- What ideas do you have for communicating with parents?
- What ideas would you have for working with a child who is not working to his potential and does not seem to care?
- What are your views on technology in the classroom?
- How do you relay the same material to students with different learning styles?
- Some students may be easier to work with. How do you plan to ensure that all students feel equally valued and respected, despite your personal feelings?

Prepare questions of your own to ask as well. The interviewer will expect it. When there is a pause in the interview process, ask "Is this an appropriate point to ask you some questions I have?" Make sure you have done your research, so you are not asking questions that are answered in the school handbook. Instead of school policy questions, ask about the expectations the administration has of its teachers. Here are a few examples of appropriate questions to ask your interviewer:

- What is the student/teacher ratio at this school?
- Do you have a teacher mentor program?
- Does this school use a team teaching approach? If so, how does is it organized?
- Is the school undergoing any major changes this year — or are they addressing any significant issues that could bring about a substantial change?
- I believe in parent involvement, and I was wondering: How active are parents at this school or within the school district?
- I enjoy using computer-integrated lessons in the classroom. What kind of technological resources does the school use — and what is available to the teachers?
- Would I have any additional responsibilities, such as working with after school clubs?
- What is the next step in the hiring process? How long before I can expect to hear something from you?

CASE STUDY: INTERVIEWING TO BECOME A TEACHER

Cynthia Rigsbee
National Board Certified Reading Teacher
Gravelly Hill Middle School
Efland, NC
tchrc@aol.com

Cindi Rigsbee is currently a National Board Certified reading teacher at Gravelly Hill Middle School in Orange County, North Carolina. In the past, she also worked as a high school English teacher, dance studio operator, junior high dance and drama teacher, middle school language arts teacher, school district new-teacher coordinator, reading teacher, teacher trainer in a staff-development office, and a middle school language arts and social studies teacher. She was named the North Carolina Teacher of the Year in 2008 and was a finalist for National Teacher of the Year in 2009. In addition to teaching, she mentors new teachers, does speaking engagements, and writes a teaching blog. Recently, she completed a book on her passion for teaching, titled Finding Mrs. Warnecke: The Difference Teachers Make. Through years of experience she has developed the opinion that some people are called to teach, while others probably should not be teaching at all.

First of all, let me say that I was not one of those little girls who lined up her dolls in a row and pretended to teach them. I didn't really see the point. We were in school all day; teaching didn't seem that exciting to me at the time. Instead, I wanted to be a Dallas Cowboys Cheerleader when I grew up. That being said, I now know that I was born to be a teacher. It is what I am supposed to do, and I truly believe that I was called to teach. I also believe that not everyone has that calling.

For some reason, however, many men and women I have encountered over the years feel they are qualified to be teachers merely because they spent some time in a classroom as a child. Along those lines, I despise hearing the quote: "Those who can, do. Those who can't, teach." Teaching is hard work. It takes patience and perseverance and years to perfect as a craft.

There are some individuals who come to teaching later in life. I didn't make the decision myself until I was in my junior year of college. So, it isn't about when you decide to become a teacher. It is about knowing that this is what you want to do more than anything and that you'll do whatever it takes to make a difference to kids. Over the years, I have had the opportunity to sit in on some teacher hiring boards. It is always instantly apparent who wants to be there for the right reasons.

If you know, beyond a doubt, that you want to be a teacher and you are ready to apply for a teaching position, keep the following in mind:

- Dress as if it matters. Most teachers do not wear full suits and high heel dress shoes to work every day. By dressing that way for the interview, however, you show that you care enough to make an extra effort. It shows that the job matters to you. Subsequently, it shows the interviewer that you are more likely to make an effort with your students.

- Display a teacher's presence. When an individual walks into a classroom and everyone gets quiet just waiting to see what comes next, I call that a "teacher's presence." Each year before school starts, I'm a little nervous myself. I have a sleepless night imagining a new group of students completely out of my control and hanging out the windows or lesson plans that aren't complete and materials not gathered. When that first day starts, those nerves may be jangling in the back of my mind, but my students never know it. I take a deep breath, raise my energy level a few decibels to show my excitement, and head into the year.
- In conjunction with nerves, do not let them affect your speaking. If you come into an interview and cannot articulate your thoughts clearly and succinctly, you probably will not get the job. How can you be expected to face a classroom of potentially unruly students day after day if you cannot even communicate one-on-one in an interview? Public speaking is the most important part of the job. If you can't speak to people, this isn't the career for you.
- Display energy and enthusiasm. Interviewers are looking for individuals who are excited about the job. If you have energy and enthusiasm in the job interview, you are more likely to have that same energy and enthusiasm in the classroom. Again, teaching is hard work. You have to have boundless energy to get the job done.
- Be prepared to showcase your work. The individuals who come to the interview with something besides their résumé and transcript always impress me. Think about what you have accomplished so far and prepare a portfolio to take with you. It can include awards you have earned, letters of recommendation, and examples of student work you accumulated during your time as a student teacher. It could even include photos of you interacting with the class. Put together a meaningful group of items that showcase who you are.
- Be passionate about the job and let your energy and enthusiasm show through.

Show Me the Money

People get into teaching for a number of reasons. They may enjoy academics, they may love working with students, or they may appreciate having their summers free. It is commonly accepted, however, that most people do not choose this profession for the earning potential. This section discloses the most recent figures concerning high school teacher earnings across the country. It also explains the many variables that affect teacher paychecks. Multiple factors affect teacher salaries. If money is a factor in your decision to accept a job, do some research before you start applying for positions.

Type of school and area of the country are the most prominent. Other factors include teacher experience, education, and subject matter expertise. Salary ranges tend to reflect the cost of living in the area. Overall, teacher salaries are generally highest in the Northeast and on the West coast. To better comprehend teacher salary ranges in the United States, see the following chart; it depicts ranges of teacher salaries in key cities across the country.

Average Median Salary Range by U.S. City

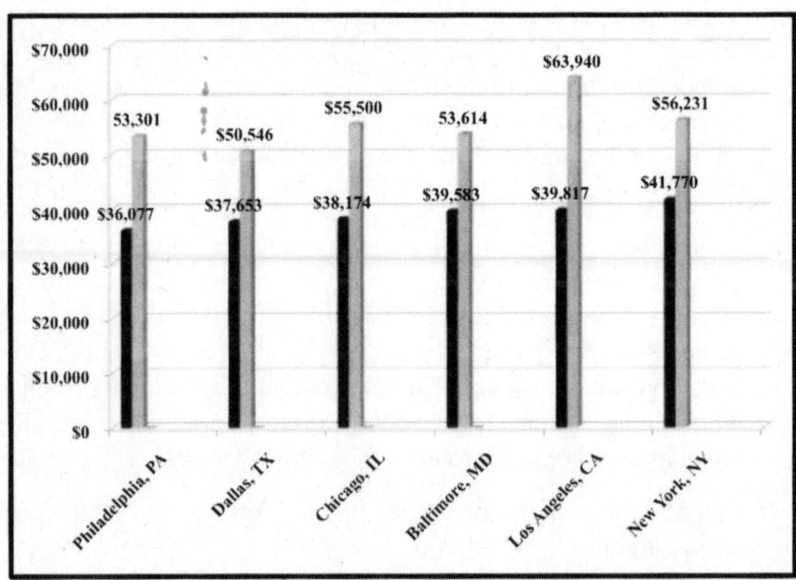

Understanding Your Earning Potential

Information pertaining to specific career salary ranges is compiled and available online by PayScale at **www.payscale.com**. The research site relates that the average earning for a new high school teacher in the United States is between $30,000 and $42,000 a year. According to the Bureau of Labor Statistics, the annual mean wage for experienced secondary school teachers in 2008 was $54,460. The pay scale Web site also breaks down the median teacher salary range by experience level.

New secondary school teachers with less than one year of experience: $29,819 to $40,818

Secondary school teachers with 1 to 4 years experience: $31,555 to $43,524

Secondary school teachers with 5 to 9 years experience: $36,563 to $50,973

Secondary school teachers with 10 to 19 years experience: $40,316 to $61,230

Secondary school teachers with 20 or more years of experience: $46,892 to $70,448

Pay scales

Payroll is handled by different departments, depending on the size of the district. It may be in accounting, human resources, risk management, or, in bigger districts, simply the Payroll Department. The Payroll Department has the specific information on pay scales and salary schedules for the district. Although statistics vary slightly in each state and district, the average teacher's starting salary is in the mid-$30,000s, according to TeacherPortal. The average salary of a tenured teacher in the United States is in the mid-$50,000s to low $60,000s.

TeacherPortal is a good reference point for an in-depth comparison of teachers' salaries from state to state. Visit **www.teacherportal.com** and click on "Teacher Salaries" for comparisons of starting pay scales and average salaries. More revealing is TeacherPortal's "Comfort Score Index." This informative index ranks teacher salaries in any given state while considering the cost of living. At publication time, the top three contenders were Illinois, Delaware, and Georgia. This is significant information for relocating job-seekers, as it shows you that gravitating toward higher-salaried states such as New Jersey or Connecticut is not necessarily where you will get the most for your dollar. TeacherPortal portrays a more accurate picture and shows where a teacher's salary will go the furthest.

Base salaries may be negotiated through the union in some districts. The amount is tied to the number of years of service and the type of contract. Below is an example of a salary scale in Palm Beach County, Fla., according to the county's Division of Human Resources. The "step" is the amount of years in service.

Salary Step	Annual / Professional Service / Continuing Contract
1	$ 36,822
2	$ 36,924
3	$ 37,485
4	$ 38,260
5	$ 38,403
6	$ 39,423
7	$ 40,379
8	$ 41,310
9	$ 42,508
10	$ 43,554
11	$ 44,870
12	$ 46,647
13	$ 48,190
14	$ 49,648
15	$ 51,152

16	$ 52,411
17	$ 53,652
18	$ 55,129
19	$ 56,618
20	$ 58,332
21	$ 60,046
22	$ 61,851
23	$ 63,687
24	$ 64,631
25	$ 65,576
26	$ 66,200
Longevity Step	$ 71,245

Pay often varies for teachers based on contract type. For example:

- **Annual contract** — An annual contract means the district has the right to renew or not renew the teacher's contract at the end of each school year
- **Professional services contract** — A professional services contract, historically known as "tenure," means the teacher has an ongoing contract and does not need to renew each year.

Many districts require you to work under an "annual contract" for three to five years before you fall under the "professional services contract." Barring any serious infractions on the teacher's part, the teacher can assume his or her job is safe from year to year after achieving a continuing contract status.

Furthermore, pay "steps" are somewhat more substantial for teachers who have acquired tenure. Note that Palm Beach County's pay raise, or "step," as shown in the chart from the first to second year is $102. From year three to four, the raise is $775. From year three to four is when a teacher initially achieves continuing contract status.

Pay schedules

Pay schedules describe the amount and frequency in which the pay is divided and distributed. Most districts pay their employees in bi-monthly installments. Teachers are often given the option of receiving their annual salaries during the ten months of the school year, or spread out over the entire 12 months to include the summer.

The pay schedule decision is a personal one. If you are self-disciplined and fiscally savvy, taking pay over a ten-month period may be is the wiser option. You can earn interest on the money you put into savings during the year. However, during your first year teaching, it is generally advised to spread the salary over 12 months. It is important to allow time in the summer for vacations, professional development, and re-energizing for the upcoming year.

Additional incentives

Some districts may offer additional pay incentives. Check to see what is offered in your area. These are a few examples of common incentives:

- **Critical Shortage Areas**: Some teaching positions are more difficult for districts to fill than others. These are known as "Critical Shortage Areas." They usually include science and math, special education, and English for Speakers of Other Languages (ESOL). There are many benefits for teachers with the expertise and education to fill these positions. Compensation may range from hiring bonuses to student loan forgiveness programs.

- **Higher degrees and certifications**: Districts regularly offer supplementary compensation to teachers with additional credentials. This may include a master's degree in a specific subject area, an ESOL endorsement, or National Board Certification. Payment may be a one-time bonus or a salary increase.

- **Travel and lower-economic school incentives**: Lower-economic and rural areas are difficult to staff. To attract quality instructors, stipends are offered in addition to regular salary as compensation for time and travel.

- **Adequate yearly progress bonus**: Adequate yearly progress is determined by statewide assessment testing in conjunction with the No Child Left Behind Act. Funding is offered to schools and/or districts that meet the goals set forth by AYP standards. How this money is spent is somewhat controversial and varies even from school to school, but it could mean a yearly bonus for you, ranging from a couple hundred dollars to more than $1,000. *Statewide assessment testing in conjunction with the No Child Left Behind Act is explained in greater detail in Chapter 10.*

- **Sick and personal days**: Teachers normally get a set amount of sick and personal days they can use during the year. Check with your district and find out whether you will lose these days if you do not take them. Some districts allow you to carry over sick days from year to year. In some cases, if these days remain untouched when it is time for retirement, the school district will calculate the amount of time saved. At that time, teachers may then receive a lump-sum parting payment upon retiring.

Other factors that affect pay

Even if you find several schools matching your perfect job criteria, there may be other factors affecting you salary offer and subsequent raises. For example:

- **The economy.** Public school teachers' salaries come out of taxes. When the economy is weak, it affects the cost of living and teachers' salaries may remain stagnant.

- **Level of education.** There are many ways to attain teaching certification. In addition, there are different levels of degree and specialization. A new teacher with a Master's degree in math or science will usually make more than a recent college graduate with a bachelor's degree in education. For example, for the Palm Beach County salary schedule, a teacher with a Mater's degree adds $3,000 to each salary step.

- **Experience.** The amount of years spent teaching affects your starting salary and raises.

- **Subject matter.** This is strictly an issue of supply and demand. For example, there is currently a shortage of qualified upper-level math and science teachers in the United States; therefore, certified teachers with proficiency in those areas may start at higher salaries.

- **Benefits.** The amount offered in benefits packages may vary. If you are single, you will most likely accept the package as is. If you are married and your spouse has benefits, you may be able to save some money by avoiding an unnecessary income deduction.

- **Union fees.** Membership has its price, another income reduction. Union involvement is another factor. Traditionally, northern states have greater involvement than many of the southern states.

- **Continuing education.** Schools may require continuing education or you may want to take classes to enhance your skill set. Some schools will pay for some or all of your continued education.

General opinion

According to a study conducted by Learning Point Associates and Public Agenda, teachers' views on compensation may depend on their own age and experience. For example, younger teachers have different expectations that their more experienced peers and they appear to have an increased sense of social responsibility. Despite that, the vast majority seems to be in agreement on one item currently debated by the Department of Education. Most teachers agree that compensation should definitely not be tied to student performance. Teacher views on compensation have changed over the past several decades. A majority of teachers agree that they should be compensated for their efforts, particularly when it comes to teaching hard-to-reach students.

Those surveyed believed that it was unfair to use student outcomes to determine compensation because many factors affect student learning that are out of their control. The study also found that most teachers admitted that they worked with some ineffective counterparts and that removing them may improve the overall environment. Many of those questioned felt that unions protected the teachers who were not effective in their jobs.

What You Need to Know About Unions

Soon after you accept a job as a teacher, you may be approached by a teachers' union representative and asked to join. The first contact will come in the form of an information packet once you start the job. Depending on the school, area of the country, and the union's presence in the district, the representative may attempt to contact you by phone or e-mail as well. He or she will continue to seek you out until you make a definitive decision. In order to be prepared, research the issue and make a decision ahead of time. There is viable information both in support of and against unions online. In addition to reading information on the Internet, discuss the issue with other teachers in your school district. Union participation varies from area to area. Some schools have close to 100 percent participation, while others have little or no participation.

What exactly are teachers' unions?

Teacher unions are paid membership groups for individuals in the education industry. The national organizations have multiple local chapters in each state. The following are some basic facts that will help you better understand teachers unions. There are two main national teachers unions for public school teachers, and there are other unions that represent specialized groups.

National Teacher Unions

- National Education Association (NEA) — founded in 1857; has 3.2 million members and partnered with the AFT in 2000. The NEA is the largest professional organization and largest labor union in the United States. They represent public school teachers and support staff. Visit the Web site at **www.nea.org**.

- American Federation of Teachers (AFT) — founded in 1916; has more than 3,000 local affiliates nationwide, 43 state affiliates, and more than 1.4 million members. Visit the Web site at **www.aft.org**.

- National Association of Catholic School Teachers (NACST) — founded in 1978. Visit the Web site at **www.nacst.com**.

Pros:

- Legal protection and good representation for collective bargaining.
- Often tied to credit unions, which provide better interest rates than regular banks.
- Assist with contract negotiations.
- In some areas, you must belong to get an improved salary after contract negotiations. If you do not belong when a union assists in contract negotiations, you may be expected to pay a fee to attain the new salary.

Cons:

- Policies can be political and may oppose your own political views.
- High membership dues; approximately $500 annually.

Paid Versus Non-Paid School-Related Endeavors

In order to supplement their income, many teachers take on additional responsibilities at the school when extra pay is offered. Many of these opportunities exist, but not all schools pay their teachers to assume these extra responsibilities, so you should inquire before agreeing to take anything else on. Additionally, as a new teacher you may not make a large amount of money, but you may want to first consider the time allocation before taking on any additional responsibilities. The following are a few jobs that may potentially augment a teacher's salary:

- Coaching after-school athletics
- Advising after-school clubs
- Becoming a new teacher mentor
- Tutoring
- Administering and grading placement exams
- Teaching summer school or home-bound programs

"At our school, teachers run almost all of the clubs. I believe this is relatively common in most Catholic high schools. There is generally a very modest stipend provided to the teachers for their time and efforts. The compensation ranges from a few hundred to a couple thousand dollars, depending on the amount of time involved. In the past, we had many coaches in the building, but not so many now. Their stipends are very low. The head coaches are the highest paid at approximately $3,000 to $4,000 a year."

— John Cominsky, religion teacher, Trinity High School

Section 2:

Start with the Basics

"The task of the excellent teacher is to stimulate apparently ordinary people to unusual effort. The tough problem is not in identifying winners: it is in making winners out of ordinary people."

— K. Patricia Cross,
educational research scholar (1926-Present)

You have accomplished your first goal by getting the job. Now you need to work on step two, which is finding, assessing, and preparing your environment. Can you find your way around the school? Do you know who to go to if you have a question? What subject will you be teaching? What desk formation will lend itself best to class interaction for this subject matter? What kinds of bulletin boards and other decorations will you put in the classroom? What kinds of files will you need to maintain and where will you put them?

These are just a few of the questions facing new teachers when they are just starting out. Section II will help you get you organized so you are ready to start teaching. Chapter 4 offers tips on what you need to furnish your classroom and where to find it. It also provides ideas on organizing your space. Chapter 5 helps you with one of the biggest challenges facing new teachers: creating the lesson plan. Chapter 6 offers advice concerning grading policies.

ANOTHER BOOK

Chapter 4

Setting the Stage

"Good teaching is one-fourth preparation and three-fourths theater."

— Gail Godwin, American author (1936-Present)

Your classroom is your own personal domain, and as long as you are in accordance with the district rules and regulations, you may decide how it looks and how it runs. Taking the extra time to create and organize a comfortable atmosphere for you and your students requires some effort on your part, especially when you are just starting out. Eventually, you will figure out what works best for you and each year it will take less effort if you remain organized.

Many new teachers are overwhelmed with where to start concerning their classrooms. This chapter provides you with the necessary information to help you get started. It includes:

- Advice on learning your way around
- A list of items you will need
- Tips on where to find school funds to pay for necessary items
- Suggestions for finding items when there is no money allocated
- How to organize the room and your school supplies
- Tips on filing and paperwork

Getting Around

Learn your way around the school. Depending on the size of the high school, this may be a simple task or it may be completely overwhelming. Check your new-hire packet to see if it includes a map of the school. If it does not, ask one of the secretaries if there is a map of the school, and if so, whether you have one. Either way, there are a number of places you need to locate immediately. They are:

- Faculty parking
- Human resources
- Main office
- Principal and assistant principal office(s)
- Attendance office
- Your classroom
- Nearest faculty-sanctioned bathroom (Some schools have separate bathrooms for student and faculty — others do not)
- Faculty lounge
- Cafeteria
- Nurse's office

These are the areas you will use first and most frequently. After that, you should acclimate yourself with the rest of the school so you can find your way around and help students find a specific location.

Classroom Supplies

The amount of time you have to prepare will depend on the circumstances surrounding your hiring. If you have the luxury of getting ready over the summer months, you can take your time setting up your classroom and getting your supplies organized. If not, concentrate on the priorities. The school and the subject matter you teach affect your supply requirements, so make sure you have all of the supplies you need.

- Determine what you need and make a list
- Assess what you already have that you can work with
- Determine your budget and/or school allocated funds
- Determine school purchasing procedures
- Place an order for supplies that must be acquired from a distance
- Purchase, find, or request other supplies, as needed
- Plan where you will put everything
- Organize supplies

Before you invest in your own supplies, find out what the school will provide for you and for the students. The best place to start is in the office. The school secretaries generally run the school. They will be able to tell you virtually everything you need to know. They will also be able to advise you on what you are permitted to do in respect to ordering materials, such as textbooks. Each school differs, depending on school type and budget. For example, many public schools provide a certain amount of supplies. Parochial schools, on the other hand, require students and teachers to provide all necessary supplies at their own expense.

The following is a basic list of items and supplies you may need to stock in your classroom. Depending on your school, the subject you teach, and what you have included in your lesson plans, you may need additional items:

- **Date planner** — You will need some kind of agenda book for school holidays, fire drills, appointments, meetings, and assignments.

- **Assorted writing instruments** — Everyone has their own preference for writing, be it pens or pencils. Whatever you use, make sure you have plenty of back-ups. Supplies tend to disappear as time goes by. In addition you own writing instruments; you may also need different colored pens for grading. If you use pencils, be sure to invest in extra erasers.

- **Pencil sharpener** — Your classroom may or may not be equipped with a sharpener for the students. Regardless, you may want to have your own in or on your desk.

- **Chalk and/or whiteboard markers and erasers** — Most schools have gone to whiteboards, either on the walls or on rollers. If so, it is nice to have a variety of colored markers for any diagrams or notes you may want to write during your lectures.

- **Scissors** — You will need these to cut out items for bulletin boards or for other class projects.

- **Scotch and masking tape** — Tape is necessary for securing items to the walls, or for putting together projects.

- **Pushpins** — Push pins and thumbtacks will secure items to bulletin boards. Make sure to ask about the school's policy about putting items on the walls of your classroom. Some schools will let you put anything you want up on the walls; others have rules about what can go up and how it is secured.

- **Stapler and staples** — Make sure you have plenty of extra staples. Not only will you use this frequently, but students will come in with papers that have not been secured and ask to use your stapler, so be prepared.

- **A ruler and/ or a yardstick** — You may these for lesson plans, for projects, drawing lines on the whiteboard, or for measuring where you want to put a poster on the wall.

- **Fasteners** — You may have a specific preference for paper clips or you may want to have an assortment of fasteners, such as paper clips, binder clips, and paper rings.

- **File folders** — First consider what you are going to file and where it will go. Do you have a filing cabinet? If so, you may need hanging folders as well, or some other means of separating types of files.

- **Labels** — You will be more organized if you label everything. In addition to using them on your files, you can use labels for identifying your personal belongings, such as an extra bookcase or lamp you may have purchased on your own..

- **Paper** — Depending on the subject you teach and the types of lesson plans you have, you will probably need a variety of different types of paper. You may need some lined, and some unlined paper. If you have a computer printer in your room, you may need printer paper. For projects and bulletin boards, you may need construction and/or poster paper.

- **Note cards** — Note cards come in different sizes and colors. Some are lined and some are unlined. Gather a variety to use for lectures, projects, and notes regarding students.

- **A hole-punch** — You may want two separate hole-punches: one three-hole-punch for papers that can be stored in a binder, and a single, hand-held hole-punch for items that only require a circular ring.

- **Calculator** — If you are a math teacher, you may want an advanced calculator with multiple functions. If not, you will still need a basic calculator for grading.

- **Correction fluid** — You will need correction fluid or tape to go over mistakes you may make.

- **Tissues** — You will want tissues for yourself and for students with colds. Many teachers ask students to donate boxes of tissues throughout the year. Some teachers even offer extra credit to students who bring them in.

- **Cleaning supplies** — You may want to keep some extra cleaning supplies on hand, particularly during cold and flu season. First check with the school sanitation engineers on school policy. Many schools are now turning to eco-friendly products and are banning certain cleaning agents.

- **First-aid kit** — You can always send people to the nurse, but depending on the size of the school and the distance between your classroom and the nurse's office, it may be a good idea to stock some simple items, such as small adhesive bandages, in your room. You may want to include some items for yourself as well, such as aspirin in case you get a headache.

Organizing Your Classroom

After you have obtained your supplies, you can start thinking about how you want to organize your classroom. You will most likely be given a set of keys to a room that is potentially messy. The following are some suggestions for approaching the task of getting it ready.

1. **Arrange the desks in the classroom first.** They take up the greatest amount of space. Doing this first makes setting up the rest of the room easier. When choosing a layout for the room, consider your teaching style, the subject matter, and the types of students you will be teaching. In a high school environment, you will want to arrange the desks in such a way that you can see all of the students at all times. If you plan to do a lot of lecturing, you may decide to choose a U-shaped alignment. This provides you with the ability to see everyone and encourages better group discussions.

2. **Position your desk based on personal preference.** There are many schools of thought on the appropriate placement for the

teacher's desk. Some teachers prefer to see the door from their desk; others do not believe it is necessary as long as they can see all of their students. Try something out — if it does not work, then you can always move it. Many teachers seem to have success with their desk in a corner that has a view of all the other desks. Another factor to consider is placing your desk and other items away from the door. This may eliminate the potential theft and other problems.

3. **Determine the placement of any other furniture.** This includes filing cabinets, bookcases, and extra chairs. If you invest in or bring in your own furniture, be sure to label it so that it is not accidentally removed from your classroom. When you place these items, consider where everyone will be sitting and where they will need to look. Try to prevent an arrangement that may block someone's view.

4. **Assess technology.** If you have computers, overhead projectors, smart boards, or other audiovisual equipment, check it to make sure they are all working. If they are not, ask the appropriate staff member what you need to do to have them fixed or replaced. Be sure to do this immediately. If the technology and maintenance departments get numerous requests of this nature, it may take a while for the repair to occur.

5. **Break out the cleaning supplies.** After the furniture is placed, wipe everything down before putting away your materials. Chances are, you will not wipe it down again until next summer when you pack up for the year.

6. **Draw a floor plan.** Before putting everything in its place, draw a plan that details where everything will be kept. Make a copy of this and keep it in your desk drawer in case you forget where you put something. This is also helpful for substitute teachers who may not know where you keep your supplies.

7. **Organize your bookcases.** This will help you find books and supplies quickly and easily.

8. **Use slat files for items you need all the time.** Consider purchasing hanging or standing slat file systems to handle paperwork that you need to access quickly.

9. **Set up files and folders with tabs.** In addition to subject specific files, you may want to organize your files by the month, season, or marking period.

10. **Address the walls and bulletin boards.** Consider the overall look and feel of the room. What subject do you teach? If you are an English literature teacher, you may want to cover your walls with pictures and quotes that pertain to the classics. If you are a science teacher, you may want to display items pertaining to the topics the students are learning.

11. **Add items as necessary.** Everything is overwhelming during your first year. As time goes on, you will think of other things you need or want to have. For instance, if you history teacher, you may want to add maps that pertain to the time period the class is studying. If you are a science teacher, you may need to update lab equipment as you change experiments. An English teacher may keep costumes or props to act out plays during certain lesson plans. When you walk by an experienced teacher's classroom and notice that it is full of books and other interesting items, remember they probably started out with blank walls and shelves just like you.

Thoughts on Student Seating

You can set up student seating in many ways: rows, groups, and squares, for instance. There are many different schools of thought on desk arrangement and student seating. The issue is largely determined by three factors:

- Classroom layout
- School policy
- Personal choice

For some subjects, such as teaching science in a lab, desk arrangement is irrelevant. If, however, you teach a subject that occurs in a traditional classroom with moveable desks, you may want to consider how you want them arranged. If your school does not have a specific policy on desk arrangement, you may move them in a formation that is conducive to your teaching style. Some factors to consider include:

- Do you plan to do a lot of lecturing?
- Do you want students to converse freely and debate topics being discussed?
- Do you plan to do a lot of work with students working in pairs or in groups?
- Will everyone need to see a chalkboard, whiteboard, or overhead projection screen?
- Does the class require interaction with other materials as in art, family consumer sciences, computer, or technology education?

The best advice is to consider your lesson plan and start out with something that makes sense. Once you have students in your room, you will quickly be able to determine what works and what does not. Most school desks are relatively lightweight and easy to push around. If you need assistance, ask the maintenance staff to help.

Eliminate formal seating charts

The concept of seating charts is primarily reserved for younger grades. In high school, it is easiest to let the students sit where they choose. Rather than waste time producing seating charts, give the students cardboard and markers on the first day. Ask them to write the name they wish to be called on the paper and tent it on the desk in front of them. You can collect the signs, but it easiest to have them keep them with their books and produce them in each class for the first week or until you get to know all of their names. There may be exceptions that require you to get involved, including:

- **IEP recommendation** — If an IEP recommends a student sit in front of the class because of hearing, vision, or attention issues, the student needs to abide by that. In many cases, the student will sit in the correct location on his or her own. In others, they may not. If that occurs, first approach the student alone and suggest he or she move to another seat. If it becomes an issue, you can move everyone in the class and make it appear as your own personal whim.

- **Class disruption** — If someone disrupts the class, or even another student, you can move that individual at that time. If certain individuals are too noisy or do not work well, together, you may move the students as you sit fit.

Storage

At this point, the room is basically clean and arranged the way you want it. Now you need to figure out where to store textbooks, learning aids, and other school supplies. Every school is different, and rooms even differ within a school. First, determine what you have to work with. Next, check with the secretaries and custodians to see if there are excess furnishings in storage. Finally, after exhausting those options, you may need to consider bringing in something from home or purchasing something inexpensive that you can use. Here is a general list of areas you will have available for storage:

- Your desk
- Bookshelves
- Tables
- Window sills
- Filing cabinets
- Storage boxes or crates

Hopefully, you will inherit a room that already has bookshelves. You will need shelving for textbooks and ancillary materials that need to be easily accessible to students. You will also need shelving for your own books, binders, and other supplies. If you are lucky, your classroom will already be set up with what you need. Newer schools may have convenient built-in shelving and cabinets.

Some schools have discretionary funds to purchase classroom furniture. If that is the case with your school, your bookkeeper may check with you to see what you need. Peruse your room and make sure you have plenty of shelving. If not, and your school makes the offer, take advantage of those discretionary funds. Teachers can never have too many shelves or cupboards. If you do not need them later and they are in your way, you can always have them sent to a storage closet.

Ideally, schools should provide each student with a book to take home and the teacher with a classroom set of the same text. That is not always the case, however. As you start learning on day one, you adjust your thinking to what is available and then you figure it out from there.

Handling Paperwork

When organizing your classroom, allocate sufficient space for paperwork. Some districts are trying to become more paperless. In those districts, you may be allocated a computer for your classroom. In those districts, you may have access to network software for lesson plans, seating charts, attendance sheets, and grading all in one. They may even have a program for digital textbook and equipment tracking. Regardless, it is still important to keep a hard copy of those records. The types of records and the amount of paperwork you keep depend on three things:

- School district requirements
- Subject matter specifics
- Personal choice

The teaching profession requires a large degree of paperwork in general. As a new teacher, this can be one of the most overwhelming areas. Here are some suggestions for keeping everything organized.

Binders

Binders allow for easy access for items that require filing, are not frequently viewed, and take up a lot of space. Use a three hole-punch for these items and store them in binders. A few examples of these items are:

- Attendance records
- Individualized student education plans
- Parent contact information
- Examples of student work
- Grade records for class, per semester
- Completed lesson plans

For easiest use, organize them in a logical sequence and keep the same system for all of your binders. If you have different systems, it may become confusing and difficult to locate items when you need them. Here are some suggestions for organizing your binders:

- *Priority* — front to back, with the most important items in the front
- *Date* — front to back, with the newest items in the front
- *Sequential* — alphabetical or numeric, depending on the item
- *Class* — as a high school teacher, you will probably teach multiple classes of individuals. In order to keep each class's paperwork separate, consider assigning each class a color.

Binders are relatively easy to store. Be sure to label them properly, so you can find what you need when you need it. Store the binders in a location that corresponds to the information contained within, and how often you need to access it. For example:

- Desktop
- Desk drawer
- Bookshelves
- Tabletops
- Windowsills
- Filing cabinets

Filing

Paperwork that does not take up as much space and does not contain student-specific information is best maintained in a filing system. Files should be labeled with easy-to-read tabs. Multiple files that are similar in nature may be grouped together. For example, you may have one hanging file containing many singular files each housing a stack of lesson plan worksheets. There are multiple ways to store files as well. You may be lucky enough to inherit some items from your predecessor. Some items may be available from a school supply closet and you may have to purchase a few items as well. Here are a few of the filing systems you could use:

- **Filing cabinets** — Preferably lockable. These are good for storing confidential files and personal belongings, such as a purse.

- **Hanging files** — Come in many sizes, shapes, and colors. Some hang over a door, hung on hook, or suspended by magnet. Check the school policy before hammering anything into a wall. If something does need to be adhered to a wall surface, contact custodial services for assistance.

- **Slat files** — Sit atop of a desk, bookcase, filing cabinet, or windowsill. These are good for items you need to access frequently.

- **Wire racks** — Similar to freestanding wire racks that can sit on top of a desk or table.

Student-Oriented Paperwork

Student records

As a teacher, you are responsible for keeping records on the students in your class. If there is a question about an issue concerning a student, you need to be able to produce documentation. For that reason, most school districts recommend keeping these records for three years after the students complete your class before shredding them. Here are a few examples of the information you need to document and file:

- Student attendance
- Parent/guardian contact information
- Record of conferences and other parent/guardian meetings
- Record of meeting or discussions of you with students
- Documentation on any disciplinary actions, such as interventions, warnings, detentions, or referrals
- Interim grade reports
- Anything requiring a parent or student signature
- Copies of certain pieces of graded work, either exemplary or items of concern
- Individualized lesson plans

Attendance

Schools require attendance records from homeroom period to determine who is present at the beginning of the day. Depending on the system at your school, this may be a hand-written form that is hand-carried to the attendance office or it could be a computer-generated acknowledgement sent via inter-office mail from your classroom computer. The school maintains these records. You will want to keep you own attendance records of the students in each of your classes. This will be important if someone misses an assignment or a test. The expectation in most high schools is that students should be responsible for getting notes, finding out the assignment, and speaking with the teacher about making up a test. The easiest place to maintain this information is in your grade book, either paper or electronic.

Student and parent contact information

The main office also maintains student and parent contact information. It is helpful to have this information available at a moment's notice. There are multiple ways to gather this information. Some schools have the information imbedded in the software and it may be attached to the student roster. Some schools maintain paper copies of student directories. If your school does not have either of these, you can collect the information yourself. You can request it from the office, or you can ask the students to fill out a form the first day of school. Keep in mind that if you ask a high school student to fill in a form with parent or guardian contact information, you may not get honest correct data.

Behavioral intervention

Another important student record to keep is a behavioral-intervention file. It is important to document issues involving student behavior. Your school may have a suggested format. This information is intended for your protection. If anyone questions your behavior or interactions with a student or guardian, you will be able to produce your notes on how you handled the situation. For most classes, you will simply need a log to record when you have called parents for positive or negative behavior issues and to track when you have assigned a detention or written a referral. Keep copies of detentions and referrals together in a file folder in case you need to provide proof at a later time. You should also keep information regarding contact with parents and guardians, especially anything that requires a signature. High school students occasionally forge their guardian's signature.

Individualized lesson plans

Any student requiring any form of classroom modification will have an individualized education plan (IEP). An IEP is a document required for any student requiring modified special education. In the United States, all children are guaranteed to a Free Appropriate Public Education (FAPE). According to the online dictionary **www.dictionary.com**, special education is "education that is modified or particularized for those having singular needs or disabilities, such as handicapped or maladjusted people, slow learners, or gifted children." Students are identified if they meet certain state and federal requirements.

The IEP is developed by team of individuals associated with the student in question. It includes teachers, parents, the student, the school psychologist, and the guidance counselor. The team will discuss the student's needs and capabilities and take them into consideration for the finalized IEP. All members of the team must sign the plan in agreement. It must include written documentation concerning the following:

- The current level of the student's academic capability
- Any issues or concerns relevant to the student's existing ability to function independently.
- Yearly measurable academic goals
- Measurement criteria for the student's attainment of these goals.
- A list of available special education services, supplies, and accommodations that will be provided to the student
- Specific written criteria for modifications that will be made for existing curriculum
- A schedule of special education services that will be provided to the student, including how and where they will be provided, and for how long
- Data concerning the amount of time the student will spend in a regular classroom and a special needs resource area, otherwise known as Least Restrictive Environment data (LRE)

- Information regarding the mandated assessments required to measure the student's academic and functional capabilities
- In cases where the student is 16 years of age or older, it must also include a plan for post-secondary school goals and transition

The IEP modifications may be simple, such as stating that a student focuses better when he or she sits in the front row. They might be more complicated, stating multiple modifications for a student with specific disabilities. Either way, you will need to refer to the information when you setting up your classroom, and again for each lesson plan. This information is confidential and must be stored accordingly.

Teacher-centric Paperwork

Class syllabus and assignment calendar

One of the first things you will do as a new teacher is to plan the material you will teach for the year. You will start with an overall topic goal, such as American history or English literature and you will break it down into a series of subtopics you plan to cover. The overview of these lesson plans is your syllabus, or what you hope to accomplish for the year. In conjunction with the lesson plans, you will determine the class assignments. These dates make up the assignment calendar. The paperwork for these to items can be kept in a binder, a file, or online. Some technologically advanced schools place all of this information online. If you work in one of these schools, you may be encouraged to develop your own Web page. If you put the syllabus, calendar and homework information online, it is beneficial for students and parents who have access to computers. When a student misses class, he can check the information online. Many districts are headed in this direction, but there are still many more that do not have these capabilities yet. If you work in one of these districts, you will need to type or write out your plans, photocopy them, and keep copies in your files.

Lesson plans

As a new teacher, all of your lesson plans will be new. As you try things, you will discover that some of them work better than others. You will want to make notations as you go along. Keep successful lesson plans for future classes. In addition to the lesson plan form, you will have worksheets, visual aids, and tests to save as well. You can store these in a binder, a file, or on your computer. If you do keep information on wither your personal or a school computer, be sure to download a copy to portable USB drive for safekeeping. Regardless of how you want to store these units or lesson plans, decide what you are going to use and prepare that storage system before you even write your first unit. You can modify your system throughout the year, but you will find your first weeks of school a whirlwind of activities, paperwork, and learning. The more organized you are beforehand, the better.

Professional employment files

In addition to student data and lesson plan information, you will have professional items you need to keep on file. Some of the items you may want to store in this area are:

- Professional development information
- Notes pertaining to meetings and in-service workshops
- Union documentation
- Copies of inter-office memos
- Employee contract information
- Copies of any documentation you wrote
- Documentation concerning extra-curricular activities you advise
- Certification paperwork
- Continuing education documentation

Keep anything that may be beneficial when it is time for your review. You will want background information on everything that shows you are doing your job, and anything that depicts that you are going above and beyond.

Technology

Depending on the financial situation of the school, you may or may not have technological equipment in your classroom. In some affluent areas, every class is wireless and each teacher has their own laptop computer. In other schools, it may still be a struggle to find an overhead projector to borrow for presentations. If you work in a district that is technologically advanced, you may need to organize your classroom around the placement of equipment, chords, and wires. Make sure everything is placed safely. Chords that run through areas where someone could trip over them are a safety hazard.

Some schools keep equipment on moveable carts in a media room. The items are signed in and out by the teachers as they need them. Overheads, projectors, smartboards, electrical carts, and other similar types of equipment may be at your disposal. If your classroom does not contain a screen, you may need to borrow one from the media center. It may be freestanding or hanging. A media specialist or custodian can assist you if it needs to be hung from the ceiling. White boards may seem as effective as screens, but this is not always the case. Using a white board as a screen prevents you from writing on the board during or even before a presentation. The slightest marks can distort projection, whether from digital equipment or an overhead projector.

There are different types of projectors available depending on your school's budget. Many schools are trending towards new advanced projection systems that provide a wide variety of visual options. If your school does not have that type of system available, they will most likely have overhead projectors. These small boxes use underlighting to project the image of the transparency placed on it up on the wall or screen. They are portable and easy to use, making them a favorite with many teachers. Often, educational transparencies for overheads will come with your text, and they are easy to use. If you have access to the overhead but cannot find transparencies, you can order blank ones and create your own or call your textbook vender, who can provide you with the ones that go with the textbook. Additionally, you can copy printed pages onto overhead transparencies — saving your students from an overabundance of paper and you from copying yet another lesson on the board. Most teachers utilize all three options for variety.

If you are not technologically savvy and need to use equipment for a lesson plan, be sure to ask a media specialist to assist you.

Those Four Walls

After you have set up your room and put away your supplies, decide what to do with the surrounding walls. In some case you may not have a lot of options — every school is different.

The following are a few potential scenarios you may encounter:

- Portable classrooms or trailers have cloth-covered walls requiring pushpins for anything that hangs on the walls.
- Older schools have walls with textured surfaces, making it difficult to hang anything at all.
- Newly painted walls may have a district policy preventing you from putting anything on them.
- A room may contain chalkboards or whiteboards on every wall, leaving little space for anything else.
- You may have a single designated tack strip for all decorations to preserve the walls.

Before you decorate your classroom, you must first understand the school policy for putting anything up in the room. After that, you must figure what you want to do with the space you have. A lot depends on the subject you teach and your own personal style. Start with what you have available to you. Do any of your lesson plans or materials come with free posters or other items you can display? After that, what other inexpensive items can you use to depict something about your class? Here are a few options to consider:

- Posters
- Student artwork or written work
- Postcards

- Magazine photos or words
- Newspaper articles
- Quotes
- Motivational sayings
- Blank newsprint that students can write or draw on

You may be able to find some items in a district teacher store. Generally, districts have a warehouse with everything from used teacher furniture to construction paper. All sorts of materials and supplies may be available to make your classroom cozy yet efficient. Check with your department chair and see whether your district has a place like this. Most districts simply require that teachers have a note from their principal in order to gain access and shop for whatever is needed. Although there may be a limit to what you can "purchase," you should be able to pick up at least the basic supplies, such as staplers, pens, pencils, construction paper, and maybe even bulletin-board borders. If your department chair is unsure, you bookkeeper will know how you can gain access to the warehouse or teacher store.

Think outside the box

That will get you started on basic bulletin boards and items that essentially can hang on the walls. It is a great place to start, but what else can you do? How can you grab your students' attention as soon as they walk in the room? Think outside of the box. Some teachers display items pertaining to favorite sports teams or places they have traveled to. Some teachers add a comfortable chair for reading or a podium for presentations. What about other decorations and props? You will spend a lot of time in this room. As long as you are permitted to do so, you might as well make it comfortable and inviting.

Budget Cuts Require Teachers to Get Creative

"East Bridgewater school officials say budget cuts will hurt education." "Town citizens raise concerns over school budget cuts." "Fort Mill school district considering major budget cuts." These are only a few of the actual headlines concerning the school budget issues plaguing everyone during the economic slowdown. The cuts have been affecting teachers for a long time. The problem has become so intense lately that many states have entitled, or are considering entitling teachers, to a tax deduction for purchasing classroom supplies. Regardless, this ongoing problem is getting worse and teachers are forced to find a way to deal with it.

Budget cuts are a real concern and it is affecting school supplies. Before you panic, however, check all of your available resources. There is actually more money available for teaching supplies than most people realize. First, talk to the principal. Some school districts allocate a specific stipend of money per teacher for supplies. After that, check with the school's Parent Teacher Association (PTA) or Parent Teacher Organization (PTO). Many PTAs and PTOs are more than happy to help new teachers get the supplies they need, providing they have the money to give. More often than not, if they do not have the money, they will hold fundraisers to raise the money.

State lottery money is supposed to go to education, and it is fine for you to ask your administrator if any of that money goes to the teachers for supplies. According to the California Department of Education, during the fiscal year of 2007-2008, the lottery generated $1.1 billion for education. It looks and sounds like a lot of money, but broken down it is only $132.20 per student. The California lottery is only 1.5 percent of all of the state's education funding, which is not much when you consider the money supported 8.329 million students. Be advised, it is best not to expect a lot of lottery money to fund teacher supplies since there are not a lot of funds to go around.

Once you determine the amount of funds that are available, consider what supplies you need to purchase. While speaking with your principal about money for supplies, you should also ask about how the items in the supply room are to be accessed. Some schools have an open-door policy where teachers may enter and take what they need. This open-door policy is becoming obsolete in many schools due to the poor economy and budget cuts.

Currently, many schools are keeping the supply room door closed and teachers must sign for any supplies taken. There is usually a limit on what you can take and how much. If you are in a school where you must sign for supplies, be sure to think before you order. The cut-off point comes faster than what you might realize and from that point on you are going to have to come up with the rest of the supplies on your own. School districts will also take orders for supplies, allotting a certain amount of money and allowing you to order from a supply list. There is usually someone in charge of the ordering, such as a secretary or custodian, and that would be the person to speak with on how much you are allowed to spend and when they will be taking supply orders.

With budget cuts getting deeper and deeper, it has become more common and necessary for teachers to revert to finding their own materials for activities. There are many places to look other than the ones previously mentioned. Parents may be willing to donate items when asked. It depends on the school district and the cost of the items you are requesting. Keep in mind the economy has hit everyone hard. Along those lines, do not expect parents or students to purchase expensive or unnecessary items for classroom projects.

Since some materials may be harder to come by than others, you may find it necessary to alter some of your planned activities. It will be helpful for you to look over your lesson plans and activities to make a list of the supplies you will need for each activity. Also, while you are making your supply list for each activity, write the date for when the activity is scheduled to take place beside it. Once you have finished your dated list of supplies needed, you have a decision to make. You can consider the supplies you will need for the first six or eight weeks and begin looking for them before school starts.

Another option is to send letters to the parents of your students and ask if they could start saving or looking for certain materials you will use. This is a particularly common practice in Catholic schools. Some teachers also offer bonus points to students who bring in items for the classroom at designated times. At the high school level, you are more likely to get students to bring in items if you offer extra credit points. Before doing this, however, be sure this is an authorized practice at your school.

Plan to obtain what you need for the first few months of activities on your own. Between the PTO or the PTA, the supply room, and your allotted money from the district, you should have a decent start to obtain what you need for the beginning of the year. You may also find useful supplies in unusual locations. For example, if you need costumes or props to act out plays, you may be able to locate them at thrift shops or garage sales for very little money. If you need cardboard boxes or packaging materials for science experiments, you may be able to find a store that can give you the items for free.

This is a perfect time to think outside the box. Enlist your high school students to be creative as well. Encourage them to use only recycled materials found around the house for class projects. Have brainstorming sessions during class to come up with ideas for finding free or inexpensive items for a specific lesson plan. Recently, Yale University department heads were asked to brainstorm creative ideas for budget cuts. Do the same with your students. Have them come up with ideas of their own on finding supplies or doing without. This is a great lesson to teach. Incorporate budget constraints into your lesson plan. Living on a budget is a very practical topic, one that not all teenagers are learning at home.

Talk to the students about reusing and repurposing items. Discuss places to find useful inexpensive items that can be used for multiple purposes. Look for items that are on sale, damaged, or have been discontinued. The following is a list of potential places to consider visiting when you are seeking inexpensive supplies:

- **Garage sales** — Used clothing and props for plays, copies of books, bookcase, filing cabinets, assorted organizational items, and office supplies.
- **Thrift shops** (such as Goodwill or the Salvation Army) — Used clothing and props for plays, used furniture, such as bookcases and filing cabinets.
- **Local newspapers** — Classified sections ads for used items for the classroom, including furniture, props, office equipment; newspapers are also good for storage, cleaning, and decorating bulletin boards.
- **Discount stores** — Inexpensive art supplies for projects and bulletin boards, furniture, and school supplies.

- **Home improvement stores** — Discounted items can be used to build projects or items needed in the classroom, such as bookcases and items for Family Consumer Science and Tech Ed classes.
- **Craft/Sewing stores** — Discounted items can be used to create for class projects and artwork for bulletin boards.
- **Local industries** — Local companies may be willing to donate older model computers and other technological items; other local business items may be donated for special projects. Call around and be specific in your requests.
- **Grocery and liquor stores** — Sturdy boxes and crates for storage or class projects.
- **Doctors and dentist offices** — Any place with a waiting room containing magazines and newspapers; ask them to save old copies for your class — for cutting out pictures and words for projects and bulletin boards.

Use your imagination everywhere you go. Keep potential activities in the back of your mind everywhere you go. If you plan to include dramatic readings in your lesson plans, you could put together a trunk of old clothes and props from thrift stores and garage sales.

Local newspapers are usually willing to give away the ends of the paper rolls because they are useless for printing. This paper is great for creating murals for history lessons. Grocery stores and local industries will be thankful to have you pick up empty boxes rather than pay someone to take them away. Printing stores and industries also have stacks of papers that are printed on one side, but can be flipped to use the other side. When you use recycled materials, you can incorporate lessons about the environment and recycling.

The possibilities of what your students can create from the materials you will gather are endless. Starting out as a new teacher, gathering the supplies you need seems like an arduous task. As you continue year after year, however, you will continue to accumulate supplies, easing the burden in the future.

Chapter 5

And So it Begins

"More important than the curriculum is the question of the methods of teaching and the spirit in which the teaching is given."

– Bertrand Russell, English logician and philosopher (1872-1970)

Getting Through the First Day of School

The first day of your first solo teaching experience is both exciting and terrifying. To minimize nervousness, be as organized and prepared as possible. A week in advance, make a list of things to go over to ensure the first day goes smoothly. Write down everything you need to attend to *prior* to the first day. For example:

- **Double-check your roster.** Make sure there have not been any last minute changes. You need to make sure you have enough textbooks and other materials for everyone in your class. Of course, if there is a last minute change, do not panic. You can always take care of it later. It is just easier to start out with all of the simple things taken care of.

- **Speaking of supplies, check the IEPs.** Some students will require special or additional supplies in accordance with their Individualized Education Plans (IEP). For example, a student who has physical limitations, health issues, or memory problems might need an extra set of books to keep at home. Make sure you have ordered or otherwise acquired everything you will need.

- **Check all furnishings.** During the process of finalizing the setup of your room, confirm that you have the correct amount of desks and chairs that are all in good condition. The last thing you need is to have someone sit on a broken chair and fall down on your first day.

- **Verify condition of classroom equipment.** Make sure everything is in working condition and that you know how to use it. Confirm any media equipment you will need for the first few weeks.

- **Review important paperwork.** During the first week of school, you and your students will handle a lot of paperwork. Make sure you have what you need and that you know what you are supposed to do with it. What gets sent to the office? What gets sent home with students? What should you keep copies of in your files? Make a checklist to prevent something critical from falling through the cracks.

- **Create a welcome packet.** Write an introduction letter. Include your name, educational background, and a few of your interest. Add contact information, such as your school e-mail address and when it would be appropriate to use it. If you have a school Web site, mention that as well. Do not give out personal information, such as your home phone number and e-mail addresses, or social networking information, such as your Facebook™ page. Doing this can create problems later, if they see you more as a friend than an authority figure.

- **Include a contact sheet.** Have a form that the students can fill in providing you with contact information concerning them and their parents or guardians. Include e-mail address, cell phone numbers, and a preferred method and time to contact the person.

- **Prepare a syllabus.** Write out a brief introduction of the class and what you plan to accomplish for the year. In addition to unit concepts, the syllabus should include a list of reference materials. For instance, if it is a literature class, some students may wish to borrow items from the library to begin reading them. The syllabus should mention fun items, such as field trips, and major papers or projects that require more work. Not all students work at the same pace. You will encounter many students who will wait until the last minute, but there will be plenty of other students who prefer to plan and organize their workload in advance.

- **Lay down the law now.** With the packet, inform students of your expectations. Include what you expect if they will miss your class, and what your classroom rules are. Spell out the consequences now. For example, "If work is not completed, your grade drops X number of points" or "Three rule infractions will earn you a detention." Whatever you decide, tell them now and stick to it. If you start out too relaxed in this area, they will take advantage of you early on.

- **Plan an introduction.** You are new to the school. Most of the students are not, but some of them might be. Plan to introduce yourself to the class and have them introduce themselves to you and to each other.

- **Review lesson plan.** Look over your first lesson plan. What does it involve for the first week? Do you have everything you need? Practice speaking in front of a mirror. It may seem awkward, but it will help you see what you look like when you are lecturing.

Everything is set up and ready to go. You have checked, double-checked, and triple-checked all of your lists. You are positive that you have not forgotten anything. You may develop a case of the first-day jitters — but relax. Most teachers admit to having this feeling every year before they go to bed before the first day of school. Join the club. It is very normal. If you truly have checked everything and feel prepared, try to expend some of that nervous energy by going for a walk, or take a relaxing bath. Do something for yourself and then try to get a decent night's sleep.

First day plans

It is here — the day you have been waiting for. What do you have planned? Some of the first day's agenda will be dictated by the school. Generally, your first period will be your homeroom. On the first day of school in high school, homeroom is usually extended. Ask the secretaries and other teachers what to expect so that you can plan accordingly. Ultimately, much of the first day will involve paperwork and introductions. By the time you have been through it for the third time, you will realize it is not as bad as you had feared. Just in case, have a plan to make things go smoothly. There is nothing worse than getting through your entire day's plan in 15 minutes. The following are a few ideas for fillers if you find yourself with extra time on your hands.

Paperwork options:

1. Have important paperwork and a welcome packet sitting on each desk as the students walk in. As they file into the classroom, they can start reviewing it or filling it out.

2. Have paper items lined up in piles on a table in the room. Some teachers prefer this. It takes a little more time as the students pick up the paperwork they need, allowing you to observe the students as they come into your room. How do they interact with each other? What kind of personalities will you have in this class?

3. Have paperwork organized and ready to go in one pile to be passed out. You can do this as the students enter the room, while asking them their names to get a head start on identifying them.

4. Have paperwork ready and do nothing until everyone is in the class and seated. At this time, you can pass it out as you are talking. Moving helps calm some individuals. Another option is to have one of the students pass it out as you are talking, taking some of the attention away from you. The option you choose depends on your comfort level. As the day goes on, you may decide to try different options to see which works best.

5. After everyone has their paperwork, go over what they need to do with it. What should be filled out? When does it need to be completed? To whom do they submit it when they are finished? If it comes back to you, make sure you have designated inboxes so you do not mix papers from different classes.

Time for introductions:

1. The easiest thing to do is talk about yourself and the class. Give the class an idea of what to expect during the course for the year. If you get nervous or tongue-tied, read the info off the sheets in your welcome packet until you get comfortable.

2. Have the students introduce themselves, or to make it more interesting, write a list of questions on the board and pair people up that are not seated next to each other. Have them interview one another and present their findings to you and the rest of the class. In addition to stating the person's name, have each person ask interesting questions, such as, "if you could hang out with one famous person for the day, who would it be and why?" The answers will tell you a lot about the individuals in your class. Plus, it is a great icebreaker for everyone.

Other time fillers as needed:

1. Find out how much the students know about the subject you are teaching. Ask questions and see who can answer them.

2. Discuss current events that pertain to your subject matter.

3. Have everyone pull out a blank piece of paper and write down one question they have about you or the class and fold them. Put them in a jar or other container and shake them up. Pull out questions at random to answer until the bell rings. Make sure you tell them that you will not answer anything deemed inappropriate.

4. Make a type of information gathering scavenger hunt for them to use amongst themselves. Make sure to have enough questions to keep them busy and tell them they cannot use anyone more than once. For example, ask them to find one person in the class for each category. Here are a few suggestions:

    - Find one person in the class who did not eat breakfast this morning.
    - Find one person who had a birthday this summer.
    - Find one person who saw a movie this summer
    - Find one person who left town this summer.
    - Find one person who speaks another language.
    - Find one person who has a part-time job.
    - Find one person who plays a sport.
    - Find one person who plays a musical instrument.
    - Find one person who read an unassigned book this summer.

Prepare a first day survival kit for yourself

No matter how organized you are the day will be fast-paced, crazy, and exhausting. Plan accordingly. Here are a few items that may help you ease you through the first day.

- **Bottle of water.** Talking all day can make your mouth dry. Many teachers start the day with a large mug of coffee, but caffeine can make you dehydrated if you do not replenish the fluids. Keep a couple of water bottles in your room in case you cannot get to a water fountain.
- **Lozenges.** Again, talking all day can make your mouth dry and might even give you a sore throat. Have some lozenges with you for emergencies.
- **Extra tissues.** It is good to have extra tissues in case you end up with multiple people suffering from colds or allergies. In that case, one box of tissues can disappear quickly.
- **Piece of fruit, granola bar, or easy-to-eat item.** This is in case you cannot get out of your room all day or find yourself starving long before lunch. A loud, gurgling stomach can be embarrassing.
- **Small sewing kit and safety pins.** These are for minor wardrobe issues.
- **Extra shirt.** This is in case you spill something.
- **Hand sanitizer and hand cream.** If you are washing your hands and sanitizing all day, you may prevent germs but you will also end up with dry, irritated hands (thus the hand cream).
- **Breath spray and deodorant.**

It is better to be over-prepared rather than find yourself wishing you had something you needed in an emergency. If you do not have space in the classroom, consider keeping small items in your desk and keeping a box of other emergency items in your car. If you will not have a car at school or close by, see if there are other areas to store items, such as a faculty lounge or locker.

"My advice is to establish the tone of the class from the first day — that way the students won't take advantage of you. Other than that, learn to be flexible. Your schedule can change at the drop of a hat and you will need to be able to go with the flow."

— Laura Cleveland, veteran teacher, Steelton-Highspire School District

Creating Lesson Plans

You have prepared the room and you made it through the first day of school. Now it is time to get into the essence of teaching: the lesson plan. Lesson planning is important for all teachers, but it is particularly important for first-year teachers. This task will take an inordinate amount of time your first year. Accept that now and you will save yourself a lot of frustration. Find time in your daily schedule to create, review, and revise lesson plans. Have textbooks, a computer, and all of your other resources available while you are working on the plans.

The good news is, once you find certain lesson plans that work, they can be reused with only a little tweaking in subsequent years. It is worth the effort you will spend. As the proverb goes, "if you fail to plan, you plan to fail."

"My advice is to be creative and put yourself in the mindset of the student. These individuals are surrounded with images from TV, movies, the Internet, music, and video games. If the subject you teach isn't exciting, think to yourself, "how would I most enjoy learning about this?" You need to think outside the box when working in this environment or you will lose the students to the distractions they have within their home. Along those lines, I like the following quote from Plato: 'Do not train children to learning by force or harshness, but direct them to it by what amuses their minds, so that you may be better able to discover with accuracy the peculiar bent of the genius of each.'"

—— Jim VanderSchaaff, social studies teacher, PA Cyber School

Choosing a format

If your school has a specific lesson plan format they want you to use, there is a reason. Embrace it no matter what you were taught in school. Some school districts have individuals hired to help teachers with lesson plans. In Pennsylvania, they use the Learning Focused Strategies (LFS) model. At Cumberland Valley High School, they employ two individuals as Instructional Coaches. It is their responsibility to assist teachers with lesson plan-related issues, such as:

- Questions concerning instructional strategies
- Expanding teachers' use of a variety of resources
- Model best-practices strategies
- Provide follow-up on professional development
- Research best practices in education
- Meet one-on-one with teachers to reflect and provide feedback

- Assist teachers in using data to drive instructional decisions at the classroom and school level
- Support the mentoring program
- Design professional development workshops

Dr. Max Thompson founded the Learning-Focused company in Boone, North Carolina. His idea was to develop an improved mechanism for lesson planning that would maximize teacher efforts and increase student achievement levels. The strategies work with all grade-level lesson planning from K-12. The strategy is currently used in more than 2,000 schools.

According to the Learning-Focused Web site (**www.learningfocused.com**), the model is based on five primary areas: Planning, Curriculum, Instruction, Assessment, and School Organization. The Learning Focused Schools Model has provided state of the art professional development and innovative instructional resources, products, and technology to more than 2,000 schools, districts, and educational agencies across the nation.

If your school district does not use a specific program or format for lesson plans, there are numerous Internet sites that provide examples. Below are a few free Web sites to visit to get ideas.

- Teachers.net: **www.teachers.net/lessons**
  This Web site includes over 4,000 free lesson plans. You can browse the plans by grade level and subject matter.

- Teacher Planet: **www.teacherplanet.com**
  In addition to a variety of lesson plans for each grade and subject matter, this site includes templates, guidelines, and advice for finding other lesson information online.

- Lesson Planet: **www.lessonplanet.com**
  Lesson Planet allows you to set up an account to access more than 150,000 pre-qualified lesson plans and accompanying materials that have been reviewed by professionals in the field.

- Teacher Vision: **www.teachervision.fen.com**
  This Web site provides ideas and examples for lesson plans and graphic organizers. It also includes worksheets that may be printed off. The information is provided by grade, subject area, and theme.

CASE STUDY: THE IMPORTANCE OF APPROPRIATE LESSON PLANNING

Cheryl Gruver
Instructional Coach
Cumberland Valley School District
Mechanicsburg, PA
www.cvschools.org

Cheryl Gruver is currently an instructional coach for the Cumberland Valley school district. She trains teachers on lesson planning, assessments, and best practices. Her prior teaching experience includes being a dance instructor, French teacher, and school musical director.

I had my first big "ah-ha!" moment my second year of teaching. My first year, I was emergency certified. I had taken education courses eight years ago and my second semester as an emergency certified teacher was my student teaching semester. (Note: Emergency teaching certification takes place when there is a shortage of teachers in a certain area. Schools will hire individuals with a bachelor's degree in these instances and allow them to teach while taking education courses to obtain a teacher's certificate.)

This meant that I did not have any current courses on lesson planning, nor did I have a co-operating teacher working with me on a daily basis. I was on my own. The assistant principal at the time gave me a tip to use when planning — plan at least three different activities per lesson.

My first year went fairly smoothly. I was teaching a language survey course that only met for one marking period. This is ideal for a first year teacher. At the end of each marking period I would reflect on my lessons and find new activities to incorporate. My unit on numbers was (what I thought) my best unit. I had many different activities in the lesson and the students really seemed to enjoy them. I continued the year reflecting on my lessons and adding to my plans.

At beginning of the following year, I adjusted my lessons from my reflection notes in my electronic copies. I then printed out my new unit binder. My lesson on numbers kept coming out page 3…4….5…6…Oh my! My lesson was activity rich, but content poor. I had some wonderful engaging activities that reinforced numbers, but the students mastered the content long before the lesson was summarized. I never stopped to assess students formatively and check to see if they mastered the information. I just kept plugging away at the activities, because they were in my plan and fun for the students.

This lesson made me stop and think about the learning targets for this unit. How does the lesson meet these targets and what activities best meet the needs of my students? I continued to keep a record of all of the activities in the unit to use when I needed to differentiate with students, but I no longer used all of the activities. I identified the three most effective, and kept them in the lesson while the rest were filed as reinforcement or differentiated assignments.

I thought to myself, "How did this happen?" I reflected immediately after teaching a lesson on its effectiveness. I used the district lesson plan format. I had three activities. AH-ha! Were these activities the best ones to move students toward the learning targets or were they simply fun? It finally occurred to me that I never went back to look at the learning targets and the goals of the lesson when I added activities. I just kept adding and never looked at the lesson as a whole.

What I took away from this moment was that it is necessary for teachers to always start with the end in mind. When reflecting, one should revisit the learning targets to ensure modifications do not affect the end goal. Teachers have a lot of curriculum to cover, so educators need to plan efficient lesson that will accomplish end goals in a reasonable amount of time.

Today, I always plan with the end in mind and as a result, I can cover more information in greater depth. Students retain information better when teachers teach for quality and not quantity. Quality planning and backwards design helped me reach more students. They helped me become a better teacher.

Elements of a lesson plan

Every teacher has his or her own unique way of teaching. Likewise, each individual has their own individual manner of creating lesson plans. A lesson plan is the manner in which a teacher organizes his or her thoughts on relaying a specific topic. They are required for each day of teaching. It is these plans that help teachers meet the curriculum set by the school district and state. You will have a general idea of what kinds of lessons you want to include when you create your syllabus at the beginning of the year. Each lesson plan needs to be carefully written out prior to starting a new unit of study.

Trying to meet the required curriculum goals can be overwhelming, especially for a new teacher, but there are ways to attain the goals without overburdening yourself and your students. While some school districts are very clear about the curriculum you are to follow, other districts are not. If your district is one that clearly expresses what you are required to teach and when you are to teach it, then be sure to get a copy of these materials and follow the set plan they have made for you. When you go to acquire these outlined materials, you will need to ask for the content standards or the educational standards. If they do not have these, you can ask for the grade-level standards or the district curriculum expectations.

There are as many types of lesson plans as there are potential lessons. Certain elements, however, remain standard. Good lesson plans should include the following:

Title: What is the lesson about? Provide a title that is self-explanatory. You may know everything about the lesson now, but you may not remember it in the future.

Lesson plan identifier: Use a date or corresponding text. The number provides you with something for easier organization and identification later on.

Curriculum areas (or concepts): What areas of the curriculum correspond to this lesson plan? What standards can be applied? The course curriculum, or regular course of study, is pre-determined by the school district. There are government standards for each grade level. For example, Geometry, Algebra I and Algebra II are pre-determined to be part of the high school curriculum. To prepare a lesson plan for one of these math courses, find out the primary learning goals for students completing this course and include them in this area of your lesson plan.

Essential question: This area of the plan relates to the standards and requirements that must be achieved based on school, state, and national guidelines. It replaced was previously stated as the lesson plan objective. Now this information is worded in question form and concerns the big ideas.

Pre-assessment (or screening): Before introducing any new material, you must understand your students' prior knowledge on the subject.

Direct instruction: Plan what information you must provide to the students during the lesson.

Student activities: This area includes detailed descriptions of your specific plans for the students. Include information on the type of activity, such as whole group, small group, or individual activity.

Summary or closure activity: Something that will wrap up the lesson, an activity that reviews what you have taught.

Materials: Plan what materials you and the students will need.

Homework and testing: Plan measurable assignments that correlate to the lesson.

Assessment: Provide different types of assessment on each lesson. This ensures that you will have sufficient information from the different types of learners.

"As a first year teacher, one of the biggest challenges I experience is creating lessons that engage all students to the point where I can figure out if they have learned what I am teaching. In social studies, sometimes it is difficult to teach without lecturing. When I lecture, I believe it becomes important to generate discussion and feedback from the students. For them to become interested, I need to make relevant connections for them. So when I do my lesson planning, I have to consider these questions:

- *How can I make it relevant to students?*
- *How can I get students actively engaged?*
- *How will I assess students as I am teaching my content?"*

— Mike Lutz, world cultures teacher, Cumberland Valley High School

Know the requirements

Before you put anything in writing, consider the standards that you must abide by. During your orientation, you will be given information on what the district priorities are in respect to the curriculum. You will also be given information on benchmarks for the national, state, and local criteria must be met in your course. Whether you are planning for a specific unit or the entire course, you need to factor in the requirements first.

1. Address the standards and requirements and put them in the lesson plan first.
2. Add in the material you would like to cover if you have time.

3. Identify material for enrichment and/or remedial needs in case it is warranted.

If you went to college to become a teacher, you undoubtedly spent hours on the topic of creating lesson plans. One of the biggest complaints new teachers have concerns lesson plans. Many people feel they are inadequately prepared for the reality of lesson planning. Others feel that they cannot use or do not need much of what was taught to them concerning lesson plans, such as the formal lengthy format. The most important thing to remember is to stay calm and not get overwhelmed. Once you get the hang of it, you will be able to create lesson plans simply, quickly, and efficiently. Until then, spend the time writing out all the information and make sure to include all of the required standards.

"Long, written out lesson plans are not helpful. You are almost never able to get it all done and then you just have to write it out again for the next day. It is better and more useful to plan a whole unit at a time that way you can just pick up where you left off the next day."

— Jen Mulhollen, itinerant learning support teacher, Cumberland Valley School District

State standards and benchmarks

In order to gain a comprehensive understanding of how to use your curriculum pacing guides and what you are expected to teach your students, you must have a comprehensive understanding of your state's standards and benchmarks. State standards are the criteria your district or state has set in place for your students to meet. In the United States, each and every state must have standards for measuring the benchmarks of student achievement. In fact, the state testing trend is based on whether your students meet the benchmarks your state has set forth for them.

Each state has its own procedure for developing standards, and the structure varies widely from state to state, so you will need to focus only on your state's standards. To view your state's standards in comparison to other states standards, refer to the Developing Educational Standards Web site at: **www.edstandards.org/standards.html**.

Steps to Creating your Lesson Plans

Once you determine the format you will be using and the elements that you want to include, you can start working on the lesson plan itself.

1. Get to know your students as quickly as possible. Once you understand their individual needs and learning styles, you will be able to incorporate the information into your lesson plan. Planning for your students' individualism creates a better lesson plan and increases your chances for successful students. Remember to consider different learning styles. Everyone learns differently and each person has areas of strength and weakness.

2. Ask yourself: "How does each student learn best? Are they auditory, visual, or kinesthetic learners?"

3. Do any of your students qualify as gifted? (Note: the United States Office of Education define "gifted and talented students as those who have outstanding abilities, are capable of high performance and who require differentiated educational programs, beyond those normally provided by regular school programs, in order to realize their contribution to self and society.") These students may have Gifted Individualized Education Plans (GIEP) to provide suggestions for their curriculum enhancements.

4. Do any of your students qualify as special needs individuals? The Individuals with Disabilities Education Act of 2006 defines "special needs" students as children who have been diagnosed with developmental delays, or any child who has been evaluated as requiring special education and related services. These students have Individualized Education Programs (IEP) to specify any modifications that need to be made to the classroom or their work.

5. Ask yourself: "Do I need to add or subtract anything to the lesson plan to aid in the success of my gifted or other special needs students?" Realize that this may be more feasible in some environments rather than others. If you have 30 students in every class and have seven periods of different students every day, it may take a longer. Do what you can.c ,0

6. Consider the objective. What do you expect to accomplish? What are the school's expectations? Ask the students what, if any, expectations they may have. At the high school level, the students may surprise you with earnest thoughts on this matter. Finally, make sure you accomplish any required standards.

7. When you create your daily lesson plan, be sure to include excess material. Include multiple possibilities and activities for relaying the information. Then, prioritize by importance and effectiveness. That way, you will not miss significant subject matter. Planning extra material also provides you with a safety net. It is better to have activities that you do not get to, rather than having a group of teenagers with too much free time on their hands because you worked through the material much quicker than you anticipated.

8. Use specific measurable objectives. Look at the benchmarks included in the standards for this subject at this grade level. You may know what you want to accomplish in the broad sense, but you need to be very specific and concrete regarding the objectives you plan to accomplish. This will be particularly helpful when you need to assess the standards that need to be met. It is also

helpful when someone else, such as a substitute, needs to use your lesson plan.

9. Be sure to include an area of differentiations. These are modifications or adaptations for students. This part of the plan relates any changes that need to be made for special needs students. This includes ideas on enrichment, remediation, and disability adaptations.

10. Specific information regarding materials is also important. It encourages you to obtain the necessary items early. This is also particularly helpful if a substitute is using your lesson plan.

11. Write down succinctly descriptive steps for the lesson. Show exactly how you will reach the objectives with the plan.

12. Include a form of lesson plan closure. This may be a return to your initial anticipated plan. By reviewing the anticipatory set, you will have a better idea about reaching your lesson plan goals. Allow students to do the summarizing by social processing.

13. Finally, write up an assessment stating whether the goals have been met. Every lesson plan may not necessarily warrant an assessment, but it is important to note if the objectives have been met with each lesson plan. Use authentic, meaningful projects, not busy work. Try to use real-life applications where possible.

Important items to consider

In addition to spending time researching the material you plan are going to teach, review the school's calendar. Dates and activities that are already built into the schedule may cause you to change your lesson plans. It is easier if you obtain this information prior to planning your lessons. The following are a few suggestions for things that you may have to work around when planning your lessons.

- School scheduled events
- Holidays
- Standardized testing
- Assemblies
- Field trips
- Observation days
- Scheduled fire drills

As you plan your daily lessons, you first need to consider the school calendar. School breaks from a normal, daily routine will affect the flow of learning in your classroom. When students are on Winter Break or Spring Break, everything they have learned previous to first day of break will be lost; therefore you should plan your lessons around your school calendar.

The calendar your school follows will determine the long breaks in your district, whether it uses a traditional calendar, a single-track calendar, a year-round calendar, or a multi-track year-round calendar. The traditional calendar is the nine-month calendar schools followed for many generations. A single-track calendar is a balanced calendar for a continuous period of instruction. Summer vacation is shortened with additional vacation days scattered throughout the school year. A year-round calendar is for schools that have session all year with long breaks intervening throughout. The multi-track, year-round calendar is used by some schools to alleviate overcrowding, and was designed for schools with a shortage of classroom space. Multi-track schools divide teachers and students into groups of approximately the same size, and each group is assigned its own schedule. A four-track year-round calendar school can extend a capacity for 750 students to 1,000 students.

When you determine what parts of the school year are scheduled for the long breaks, you will want to schedule the more in-depth, longer lesson plans between these breaks. In a traditional school, you will have 180 days to teach your class, but on average you will lose approximately 30 of those days due to assemblies, special events, and/or visits or other interruptions. It may be easier if you organize your lesson plan as a unit plan. Take each unit and break it down into daily lessons by including the following:

- Identify your objectives.
- Determine what materials you will use to teach said objectives.
- Plan alternatives for absent students, especially if your lesson plan can be hard to make up.
- Decide how you will assess your students on these lesson plans.

Consider your calendar with all school breaks marked off, then pencil in when your units of teaching will begin. This way, you will be able to use your calendar when writing your lesson plans in your plan book.

By taking the time to determine the objectives you want your students to learn, you will find you are reaching your set curriculum in a more organized way. Some schools ask their teachers to follow guidelines the federal government publishes. If this is the case, administrators will let you know during meetings scheduled before school begins. In planning your daily lessons to meet the set curriculum, you will also want to remember the state-mandated testing that takes place in your school.

"The first year is really difficult. This year, I have had difficulty finding time to plan lessons and grade assignments while having to worry about all of the other small issues that did not pop up while I was a student teacher. Prioritize what needs to be done. I have placed lesson planning as the most important issue that needs to be addressed. Grades will get done when the lessons are planned. Keep your nose to the grindstone in the first year, celebrate the small achievements, and do not let yourself get dragged down by the difficulties you encounter. Everything is a learning experience and it only gets easier from here."

— Mike Lutz, world cultures teacher,
Cumberland Valley High School

Putting it into practice

Some school districts require you to list the standards met on every lesson plan you use. This is another good reason to list your objectives for your lesson plans. It is important become familiar with the material you are teaching your students. You will find that, with all you have to do in one day, there is not nearly enough time to prepare for tomorrow's lesson plan. But your lesson plan does not need to be a long, drawn-out explanation of each step — you can make your lesson plan brief and use your own personal shorthand when doing so. Although the college professors taught you that the long, explanatory lesson plan is the proper way, before your first year of teaching is over, you will find yourself thinking it is a waste of valuable time.

Some school districts require their teachers to turn in their lesson plans, and if this is the case for you, you may want to add a few lines of explanation. Most schools do not mind brief plans as long as it is understandable in the hands of a superior.

How you write your daily lesson plans is up to your discretion. The best advice is to write them however works best for you. While some teachers will write out their lesson word for word, others will use one to five sentences and naturally fill in the gaps while teaching the class. Whichever style is best for you is fine as long as you know the material and can answer questions your students ask. It is fine to be surprised by a question you have no answer for and learn the answer to that question with your students, but if you do not know the material and have no answers, you are going to look bad, lose the respect of your students, and be an ineffective teacher.

While you prepare your plans, you will want to decide how you will assess your students to determine if they have learned the material. When you have decided which method of assessing you will use, whether through testing, an activity, or a recital, you can then look at the lesson plan again and see if it will prepare the students appropriately. If the lesson does not teach the student the material needed for the assessment, you will need to either change the lesson plan or your material in the assessment. Keep in mind that lesson plans and assessments go hand in hand. *For examples of possible lesson plan formats, see Appendix 2: Easy-to-use Lesson Plans.*

Over the course of five years of teaching, I have learned that the best thing you can do is to over-plan until you know how long each class takes with the different activities.

— Rachele Dominick, advanced placement English teacher, Cumberland Valley High School

Common Planning Errors by New or Inexperienced Teachers

Despite the amount of time spent on lesson planning in college, most new teachers are unprepared for the reality of this type of planning. It takes time, thought, energy, focus, and concentration. Even the most experienced teachers will have lesson plans fall apart for one reason or another. No matter how tedious lesson plans seem to be, there is a set of necessary elements for a reason. The following is a list of common lesson plan mistakes that often occur to first year teachers.

1. Forgetting the importance of writing course, unit, and daily plans in entirety. Thinking they can "wing it" once they get into the classroom.

2. Despite the importance of mandates, ignoring or inadequately preparing for national, state, and district standards.

3. Mistakenly preparing only a list of activities instead of a full-fledged lesson plan.

4. Lecturing non-stop to the students for the entire lesson and forgetting to incorporate other elements.

5. Moving over the material too quickly, forgetting that many students need to be taught in different ways.

6. Eliminating elements that provide for different learning styles.

7. Forgetting to make provisions for adaptations.

8. Spending too much time on one aspect of the lesson or unit and failing to prioritize.

9. Forgetting to assess the prior knowledge base of class and individual students before starting a lesson. This creates problems if a piece of the necessary knowledge base is missing. It also prevents the teacher from helping the students to make connections with previously learned material. It can also be a problem if students already know the material and you waste time being repetitive, thus boring the students.

10. Failing to use elements that evoke critical thinking skills from the class.

11. Inadequately preparing the students prior to testing students.

12. Forgetting to provide sufficient practice opportunities for using the material.

13. Eliminating homework and other assessment opportunities that help students master the material prior to testing.

14. Neglecting to prepare required materials ahead of time.

15. Forgetting to sufficiently fill out lesson plans that a substitute could easily follow.

16. Forgetting to use formative assessment to guide instruction.

Chapter 6

Making the Grade

"Correction does much, but encouragement does more."

— Johann Wolfgang von Goethe,
German writer and philosopher (1749-1832))

The true test of the effectiveness of your lesson plans comes in the form of grading. Grading is the formula teachers use to assess if the students understand the concept. Merriam-Webster defines grade as "a mark indicating a degree of accomplishment in a school."

Grading is the assessment part of your lesson plans. In a perfect world, if you took everything into consideration and taught the unit effectively for all different types of students, the majority of them would succeed on any form of measured testing. It is not a perfect world, however, and no matter how hard you try to incorporate everything you have learned, there is still a good possibility that a percentage of your students will fail to grasp the lesson when they are tested. Why is this? You are taught in college to accept the differences and to plan your lessons accordingly so that no one is left behind. The truth is that you can never plan for all the variables. You can be patient, observant, and sympathetic when you know what the variables are, but you will not always be able to know what they are. Sometimes you may be able to see that there is a problem, but you may not always be privy to the information you would need to help a student. High school students, unlike elementary students, are not always forthcoming about what is going on in their lives. For example:

- You may not always know what is going on at home.
- You may not always know if the student is getting enough sleep or adequate nutrition.
- You may not always know if homework is incomplete because the individual did not want to do it, or if there is a valid reason.

In addition to student variables, some subjects are more challenging than others to grade, as some concepts are less concrete than others. For example, interpretation of art and literature is much more subjective than knowing the elements in the periodic table and what they are used for. Neither is more or less important than the other; they are just different. This chapter provides advice that will help you in assessing your students. It includes information on the following:

- *Learning styles* — use this information to help plan your lessons. How your students learn will affect how well they understand the lessons and how they do on assessments.
- *Assessments* — review the types of assessments and how to use them in your classroom. Read a case study of a first year high school teacher's grading challenges.
- *Rubrics* — learn how to effectively use this assessment tool.
- *How you are graded as a teacher* — understand how your student's performance will affect you and how you will be assessed as a first year high school teacher.

Learning Styles

Lesson planning and assessment are the two main components of teaching. Many college courses cover these topics, but since they are somewhat intangible concepts, it is difficult to grasp until you are teaching in your own classroom for the first time. One factor that helps in the areas of lesson planning and assessment is the concept of learning styles. By the time students reach high school age, their learning styles and work ethic are well formulated.

Observing your students and taking these concepts into consideration will help you with planning and assessment.

There have been many theories and models over the past four decades. Two of the theories are particularly helpful in basic lesson planning. The first of those theories concerns learning styles. The VARK model (described below) is the most commonly used model. It essentially states that based on neurolinguistic programming, each individual falls into a basic learning style group. For most people, one of these styles is usually dominant and another may be secondary. When you have a student who appears to be struggling, consider the following concepts. Perhaps you can modify the way you deliver a lesson or reconsider the way you have been assessing that individual.

- **Visual learners**: These individuals learn best by seeing. They are very aware of nuances in body language and facial expressions. These students enjoy visual displays and are more likely than their counterparts to take copious notes. Visual learners will naturally gravitate to the front of the classroom. As a teacher, you will reach them by using visual aids, such as diagrams, handouts, and overhead transparencies. These students do not have difficulties making up work, because they can pick up the information easily from the textbook, notes, and handouts.

- **Auditory learners**: If you have students that do well in class, but do not appear to take a lot of notes when you are lecturing, they may be auditory learners. They will understand the material better by paying close attention to you, rather than by writing things down. They are very aware of voice pitch and variation in tone of voice and volume. To these individuals, *how* you say something is as important as what you say. They will enjoy lectures with class participation. Auditory learners do well when they are in your class, but they may have difficulty making up work if they are absent. Reading over someone else's notes will not be as effective. If you have an auditory student with special needs, it may be beneficial to allow them to use a tape recorder for the lectures. Listening to it again will help them, more than studying it out of a textbook. Auditory learners tend to talk more than the other learning styles and have greater verbal tendencies.

- **Reading/Writer-preference learners**: Students with reader/writer preferences learn best by rewriting their notes or copying material out of a textbook to study. Re-writing what they read programs the information into their memory. If a few of your students seem to study a lot by reading the material and listening in class, but cannot seem to transfer what they learned at test time, it may be beneficial for them to copy over their notes or make an outline. Write key facts on the board or display information on an overhead transparency for these students to copy.

- **Kinesthetic learners**: These individuals tend to have the most difficulties in a traditional classroom. Kinesthetic learners learn best in a physical manner and do not like to sit still for long periods of time. They need to move around. They learn best by doing and touching. Sitting in a classroom listening to a lecture for 45 minutes is painful for these individuals. To reach this type of student, incorporate visual aids that can be passed around. They would also enjoy creating a physical project in class or acting out some part of the lesson.

Some students are more obvious in their learning style than others. To help you gauge the learning styles of your students, ask them this question: *If you needed to determine how to get to a friend's house, how would you do it? Would you:*

a. Ask for directions and remember what you were told.
b. Find directions online and print off to take.
c. Write down the directions.
d. Follow someone else who is going there.

The way a person answers is a good indication of his or her learning style. Consider the first word in each answer:

a. "Ask" indicates an auditory learner
b. "Look" indicates a visual learner
c. "Write" indicates a reader/writer-preference
d. "Follow" indicates a kinesthetic learner

If you listen carefully for key words in how students would handle a simple task, you will be able to tell what their learning styles are. You can also have the students take a written quiz or an interactive quiz online at LDPride.net: **www.ldpride.net/learning-style-test.html**.

Another widely accepted learning model is the theory of multiple intelligences. In 1983, Harvard University professor Howard Gardner developed the theory as an argument to the accepted manner of assessing people's intelligence. His theory is that there is not only one measurement that identifies human ability, but seven separate forms of intelligence. In other words, if someone does not appear to have a strong inclination in one area is not an indication of his or her intellectual capabilities. The following chart illustrates the theory of multiple intelligences.

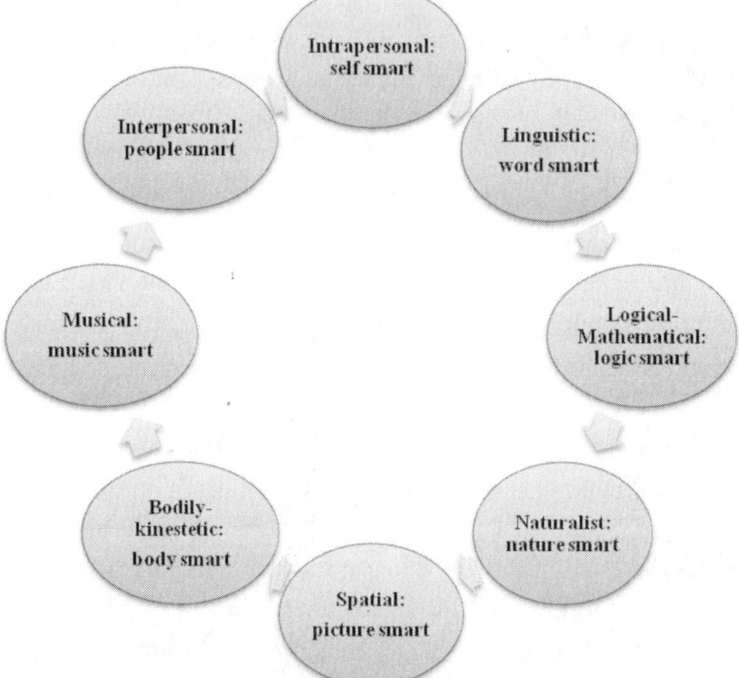

The eight types of multiple intelligence are:

Linguistic Intelligence: These individuals are "word smart." They have exceptional vocabularies and speak eloquently. These students will excel at speaking in front of the class, using humor, debating, and remembering information that is told to them.

Logical/Mathematical Intelligence: These students are "logic smart." They are skilled in applying logic and reasoning. These individuals will enjoy solving math equations, doing science experiments, and deciphering logic problems.

Naturalist Intelligence: People with these capabilities are "nature smart." These students will be most apt to recognize and categorize things in relation to the environment. According to Gardner, this intelligence pertains to "the ability to recognize and classify plants, minerals, and animals, including rocks and grass and all variety of flora and fauna." These students enjoy grouping and categorizing. (Note: This category was not one of the original seven intelligences. It was added later.)

Spatial Intelligence: These students are considered "picture smart." Their abilities will include completing puzzles, understanding charts and graphs, and drawing.

Bodily/Kinesthetic Intelligence: These people are "body smart." They prefer to express themselves by moving. They are very coordinated and excel at sports and other physical endeavors. Projects that allow them to use their hands would be preferable.

Musical Intelligence: These are the "music smart" students. Musical learners respond best to music. Memorizing something in song form is very helpful.

Interpersonal Intelligence: These individuals are "people smart." They are sensitive to others around them. They are always trying to ascertain everyone else's point-of-view. They do not like confrontation and do best when everyone is cooperating. These individuals work best in a group.

Intrapersonal Intelligence: Students with intrapersonal strength are "self smart." They are more analytical and reflective than others. They may get caught up in their own daydreams and feelings. These students are most effective when they understand the benefit the material has to them.

In addition to unforeseeable student factors, there is the issue of subject matter. Not all subject matter can be graded objectively. For example an art project must be graded more subjectively than a test on the periodic table of elements. As a new teacher, how should you develop grading policies that will work? First of all, remember you are a new teacher. This is one of the most challenging areas for a new teacher because there is no one concrete formula to follow. Every subject is different and every teacher has his or her own approach to grading. As you will find with most everything else this year, there is a lot of trial and error involved with the first year of teaching. So, where should you start? Begin by understanding the terms and trends in education today.

Assessments

Although students, teachers, and parents still refer to the grades on a paper test or project, the term used in education today is "assessment." Assessment is a form of appraisal and evaluation essentially used to determine the value of the item in question. In the world of education, the value comes from determining whether the student understood the lesson, and to what degree.

As an aspiring teacher, you may already be familiar with the four primary distinctions of assessment. They are:

- Formative and Summative
- Objective and Subjective
- Referencing
- Formal and informal

Grading, or assessment, is and always has been subjective. In an attempt to keep things fair and equal, there are high school grading policies in place. In order to comply with mandates, such as No Child Left Behind (NCLB), public school districts have move toward standards-based assessments. To use this system correctly, you must understand the difference between formative and summative evaluation and teaching.

- **Formative assessment** — Develops student understanding and mastery of the material. Completed homework assignments, classwork, and group interaction fall into this category. Formative assessments, also called educative assessments, continue throughout the lesson plan. For example, this may occur in the form of a teacher providing feedback to the student during the class. If formative assessment is used correctly, the teacher can gauge student progress and offer assistance when and if it is needed. Challenges still arise when some students grasp the material more quickly than others. That is why you need to account for enrichment in your differentiation.

- **Summative assessment** — Demonstrates the student's individual mastery of the lesson as determined by tests, quizzes, papers, and other projects. Summative assessments evaluate the student's grasp of the concept at the end of the lesson plan.

The point of formative and summative assessment is to have your students' grades truly reflect their mastery of the subject. As a new teacher, it will take time, practice, and a lot of trial and error until you achieve the correct balance of measurement in this area. The following are some suggestions to help you in the meantime. Consider the following:

- The point of grades in using formative and summative assessment is to show mastery. In order to achieve the desired results, you as a teacher need to clearly articulate and document what you consider to be a clear indication of mastery.
- Use rubrics to show the student what is expected for the assignment and how it will be graded.

- Grades are intended to reflect student progress. Along those lines, you should never use grades as a punishment or as a reward.
- Formative assignments are intended to help you gauge the class and individual student's understanding of the topic. Be sure that any assignments in this area should only form a very should be a very small percentage of the overall grade.
- Summative assessments should form the majority of the lesson plan grades, and subsequently the overall grade for the marking period.
- Some teachers include class participation and overall effort into their grades. This is very subjective and cannot be measured objectively. It also does not necessarily indicate mastery. For that reason, this really should not be used in this method of grading.
- Since the primary focus of formative and summative grading is to ensure each individual student has understanding and mastery of the subject, group work should not be a portion of the student's overall grade.
- In working toward improving the understanding level of each individual student, test retakes should be allowed within reasonable boundaries that are established up front.
- Formative assignments should be intended for the express purpose of assisting students and allowing them to practice the skills they need to master.
- Anything that you assign as work should be graded to provide feedback to the students on their progress.
- For accurate summative results, you as a teacher you have multiple tests, projects, and papers depicting mastery in all the skills that relate to the topics of the unit.
- Final overall grades should be primarily summative. If true mastery is achieved, the grades will reflect consistency.

CASE STUDY: LEARNING TO GRADE

Mike Lutz
World Cultures Teacher
Cumberland Valley High School
Mechanicsburg, PA

Mike Lutz is currently experiencing his first year as a high school teacher. He teaches two levels of the course: one academic and one college prep. At the time of this case study, he was in the third marking period.

Every school has its own report card and grading practices. For example, Cumberland Valley uses percentages and weighting systems. The school gave a general explanation of the grading policies when I started, and I felt it was sufficient for me. My biggest challenge as a new teacher has been trying to find a consistency in my grading procedures. With all of this material being so new to me, is it difficult to know what I expect as a high quality assignment. Consistency in grading will come in time. Until then, I attempt to make my rubric as specific as possible, so if questions arise about grades, I am able to answer specific concerns.

The school did offer guidance for grading writing assignments at our first year training. I learned a lot about rubrics in college and how important it is to make them as specific as possible. However, I have found that any assignment I grade is very difficult in the first year. You do not always know what to expect in the answers you receive. As with many things in teaching, I believe the more practice you get with grading specific types of assignments, the better you become. Grading assignments next year will be easier because I will know be able to tell the difference between good answers and poor answers.

When I feel that I want students to demonstrate their understanding of the basic information, I assign a test or a quiz. I assign a project or a paper when I want students to think critically about what they have been learning in class. I have assigned projects that incorporate drawing skills, computer literacy, and creative writing. Creating projects can be a great experience, but it occasionally becomes a challenge to create an assignment that is understandable, creative, practical, and also fits with the curriculum that we are assigned as well. In my first year, I have found that it is difficult to constantly think of creative assignments when so much time is spent learning the material that I have to teach on a daily basis.

There is not a huge difference in teaching the material at the two different levels. Sometimes all it involves is spending more time explaining the assignment. Other times, it involves giving more feedback as they work on the assignment, or providing more class time for it to be completed in school. In teaching the lower level class, the most important thing to remember is that they just need someone to listen and understand where they are coming from. If you can be that person, they will be so much more responsive to you as a teacher.

When a student is struggling in my class, I usually take the time to speak with the student after class. I always preface the conversation with asking, "Is everything OK?" I make it a point to let the students know they are capable of passing and that I am here to help them with what they need. If this does not work, I will talk to other teachers who have that student to see if they are having issues in other classes as well. Then will ask how they have approached the issue. Since I am still new, if I need to contact a parent or guardian, I seek advice from colleagues to find out how I should address the issue.

Cumberland Valley uses eSchoolbook, an online grading system. It has definitely made my job easier. I am personally responsible for posting my grades. The downside is some parents will check the Web site daily and will question when a specific assignment will be posted. As a first year teacher, it is extremely difficult to grade assignments in a very quick manner. I get them done as soon as I can, but I place my highest priority on planning and preparing my lessons.

One of the biggest challenges I had that I did not expect was learning how to deal with students who need to get caught up on the material. There have been several situations this year where I needed to help students who were new, on vacation, or out sick catch up on over a week's worth of material. My advice to other new teachers is to have students find homework partners who came help them with notes and assignments that they may have missed.

What is more complicated is trying to allocate work in advance for someone who knows they will be out for a week for vacation or another reason. Since I am still working through my first year of lesson plans, it is sometimes difficult to know in advance what I will be covering and how long it will take. In this situation, I have given the students worksheets from the textbook so that they can have some work related to the concepts I plan to cover. I think this will be easier in future years, when my lesson plans have been more in place. This year, I have had to be very flexible in these situations.

All About Rubrics

The primary mechanism for grading in the formative and summative assessment methodology is the rubric. This grading tool is a method for clearly stating the teacher's objectives in any given assignment. It explains what grade the student can expect based on how well he or she masters the objectives. The written explanation is written by the teacher and given to the student prior to the paper or project so they know what they will be graded on.

If you recently graduated from college, you are probably familiar with rubrics. If you are unfamiliar with them, a rubric is generally created by dividing apiece of paper into blocks. Each block represents a set of criteria and standards pertaining to the assignment. It is actually a very simple tool. It takes opinion and subjectivity out of the equation. Teachers enjoy using rubrics because they take a lot of guesswork out of grading, which saves them time. The teacher checks off the squares that coincide with the students work and the grade manifests itself. Rubrics are used for all subjects for any assignment that is graded. The following is a picture of a blank rubric form:

MATH RUBRIC

Name: ____________________ **Date:** __________

Grade: __________ **Teacher:** ____________________

	Criteria				Value
	1	*2*	*3*	*4*	
Explanation	Misses key points.	Explanation is unclear.	Good solid response with clear explanation.	A complete response with a detailed explanation.	______
Use of Visuals	No diagram or sketch.	Inappropriate or unclear diagram.	Clear diagram or sketch.	Clear diagram or sketch with some detail.	______
Mechanics	Major math errors or serious flaws in reasoning.	Some serious math errors or flaws in reasoning.	No major math errors or serious flaws in reasoning.	No math errors.	______
Demonstrated Knowledge	Response shows a complete lack of understanding for the problem.	Response shows some understanding of the problem.	Shows substantial understanding of the problems, ideas, and processes.	Show complete understanding of the questions, mathematical ideas, and processes.	______
Requirements	Does not meet the requirements of the problem.	Hardly meets the requirements of the problem.	Meets the requirements of the problem.	Goes beyond the requirements of the problem.	______
				Total:	

Teacher Comments: ____

____

____

____

Your school may have programs for creating rubrics. If not, there are numerous sites online for creating rubrics. They are all very easy to use. You can start from scratch, or you can find a sample that is for a specific subject or task. The Web sites post examples for all different subjects at all grade levels, for multiple types of graded assignments. The following are a few teacher-recommended sites:

- Rubrics for Teachers (**www.rubrics4teachers.com**) provides a large variety of blank rubric templates for multiple subjects and grade levels.

- TeAch-nology (**www.teach-nology.com/web_tools/rubrics/secondaryrubrics.html**) is an online teacher resource for lesson plans, printables, and rubrics. It assists teachers in creating custom rubrics.

- Makeworksheets.com at (**www.makeworksheets.com/samples/rubrics/custom.html**) requires you to become a member for a fee. Members can access rubric templates or create custom rubrics.

Using rubrics helps students evaluate their own work. It clarifies the teacher's expectations. To use your rubrics in your class, follow these steps:

1. Prepare and show the students good examples of the type of work you expect from them. Create examples depicting poor quality. Let the students compare the quality of the work.

2. After showing the examples, list the criteria that will be used in the rubric. Discuss what qualifies as good work in the highest expectation categories. Ask for student feedback as you go, involving them in the process.

3. One the criteria for the highest expectations are established, discuss the gradual variations of that quality. In other words: Great

work includes all aspects of the project and exceeds the expectations; good work meets all the criteria; fair work meets some, but not all, of the criteria; and poor work does not meet any of the expectations of the assignment.

4. To determine if the students understand the assignment and the expectations, ask the students to test the rubric on sample assignments you create. This also allows you to determine if they thoroughly understand the expectations of the assignment. As the students use the model, have them make any changes to their own work. This step allows you to use formative evaluation to see if there are student difficulties with understanding the expectations.

5. After they modify their work, ask them to exchange work with another student for peer evaluation and feedback.

6. At this point, students will make additional modifications based on the peer review. Have students revise again based on the feedback they receive.

7. The final step is teacher assessment. This is the summative step. Use the same rubric students used during the revision process and assess their work. If students follow each step, the final product should be much better. The majority of students will at least meet all the expectations, and a number of students will exceed them.

How You Are Graded as a Teacher

Students are not the only ones who need to be concerned with assessments. As a student teacher, the cooperating teacher and other student teacher supervisors observed you. As a new high school teacher, you will again be subjected to observation. High school principals, administrators, and department chairs may all perform the evaluations for new high school teachers. They sit in on classes and observe the teachers at three different points in the year. Depending on the school district, multiple observations generally continue for the first few years of teachers. After that, you will still have observations, but they will only be once a year.

There are two types of observations: scheduled and unscheduled. Scheduled observations occur when the principal or other administrator notifies the teacher that he or she is going to be coming into the classroom for an observation visit. These allow the teacher to prepare to be observed. You can plan your lessons accordingly and tell your students what to expect. The other type, unscheduled visits, can create anxiety for even the most seasoned teacher. For a new teacher, the thought of a school administer dropping in for an unscheduled classroom visit is truly terrifying. After all, everyone has a bad day, and there is always a chance for an unexpected visitation to occur on one of those days.

Most schools try to incorporate both types of observation in to the evaluation process. By visiting the classroom at both scheduled and unannounced times, the administrators get a more accurate picture of what kind of teacher you are. It shows how you are able to organize and orchestrate a planned lesson; it also depicts how you hold up under the pressure when nothing goes as planned. In addition to seeing how you handle yourself and the class, here are a few of the things administrators are looking at during the observations:

Curriculum

- Content quality
- Appropriateness of material
- Organization of lessons

Instructor Effectiveness

- Presenting material
- Explaining concepts
- Garnering student interest

Student's Response

- Amount of student participation
- Quality of student participation

The thought of being observed causes some new teachers to panic. If that happens, stop and breathe. You were hired because you had the necessary skills to do the job. You are capable. Take a second to regroup and continue teaching as if no one was in the room to observe you. Continue to teach without getting flustered, and you will more apt to control the environment. If you stay calm, you will get better student participation. If you get nervous, they will get nervous.

Section 3:

Using Your People Skills

"Education is the ability to listen to almost anything without losing your temper."

— Robert Frost, American poet (1874-1963)

This section of the book offers advice on using effective communication skills, such as introducing yourself to your students, teaching a wide array of ability levels, and earning the respect of a difficult group: teenagers. It offers tips on working with students, parents, administrators, and other staff members.

A number of potential scenarios and solutions are also included, as well as advice from dozens of students, parents, and other teachers who provided input. The assistance of peers and support staff can be valuable when you are just starting out. Learning who you can turn to when you need guidance is important step for any first year teacher.

CASE STUDY: WORKING WITH DIFFERENT PEOPLE

Kathy Heisler
Cumberland Valley High School
Teacher of Psychology (28 years) and Special Interest (four years)
KHeisler@cvschools.org

Kathy Heisler had her first job as a substitute teacher during the 1978-1979 school year in western Pennsylvania schools. The following year, she taught in the Mechanicsburg Area School District in Pennsylvania. In 1980, she was hired as a full-time psychology teacher at Cumberland Valley High School in Mechanicsburg, Pennsylvania, a position she held for 28 years. In the past four years, she has worked with gifted students as a special interest teacher at Cumberland Valley. Heisler's Case Study provides advice for new teachers on what she has learned over the years working with different types of people.

If possible, get to know your students and their histories. I would suggest doing this especially if the student appears negative, disinterested, or disruptive. Getting to know the student puts the pieces of the puzzle together. Students generally are not nasty just to be nasty; there are reasons. The social studies class that I taught for so many years was on the lowest academic level. I had the "worst" kids in there, as far as discipline issues were concerned. I loved teaching them how to behave and treat one another with respect. It was an awesome challenge that I embraced. Some weren't very bright, had crazy home lives, worked 40 hours a week at a job outside of school, had poor attendance records, and many other issues. I learned how rough life can be for a segment of our student population. Many of those students really touched my heart.

When you communicate with others, try to phrase everything you say in positive terminology rather than negative phrasing. Here are some examples:

1. Say "Get to class on time" rather than "Don't be tardy."
2. "Bring your book" as opposed to "Don't forget your book."
3. "Try to see the positive" versus "Don't be negative."
4. "Strive to succeed" instead of "Don't fail."

Taking the positive one step further, try to reward good behavior instead of punishing bad behavior. Catch students doing something good and call their attention to it. Everyone loves to be recognized. At the end of every school year, I had a two-day awards event. In the last month of school, I would have all the students write comments about their fellow students in the class. The only requirement was that the comments had to be positive. I collected and compiled the comments. Then I gave each student his or her own collection of comments from the group. Of course, there would always be one or two students whom everyone would comment on.

On a few rare occasions, a student may not have received any comments. In those instances, I would make up a few comments and put them together for the student. The point is to make everyone feel good about him or herself. I had reward certificates printed and filled them in for each student. I tried to talk about each student for two to three minutes. They came up to the front of the room and I hugged them as I gave them the certificate and student comments. The students loved this and looked forward to it. Instead of the last few days of school being hectic and crazy, the students sat and listened as they each were given their two minutes of fame. When I run into former students today, some of them still mention the award they received.

Here are a few of my favorite assignments from over the years:

1. *Food Assignment.* For back-to-school night, the hallway was always decorated with submissions from students concerning my food assignment. The assignment was for each student to find a picture of a food that represented his or her personality. Then they had to write a short descriptive essay describing how their personality related to the food. The day the assignment was due, I would read them aloud to the class and ask the students to guess who I was reading about. It was always a colorful assignment and the parents always stopped in the hall to read them.

2. *Role Model Assignment.* I combined this assignment with teaching about Albert Bandura's social learning theory and the importance of role models. I had each student write a short essay describing an important role model in his or her life. The assignment would also require them to read it aloud in class. That usually took several days and sometimes students got emotional. They would write about parents, deceased grandparents, athletes, and friends. The

second part of the assignment is the part I enjoyed most. I offered the students extra credit if they agreed to allow me to send the essay to the role model. I had a form letter that I sent out with the essay explaining the assignment. I especially liked it when a student wrote about a parent and agreed to let me mail the essay home. I received overwhelming positive responses from people who received the essays. Students would often come to class and tell me their mother cried when she received the letter. I loved that assignment.

3. *Life Skills Assignment.* ("Life Skills" is a set of classes for kids with special needs. Another optional assignment I gave each year consisted of having students work with the Life Skills kids during their study halls and write a reaction paper on what they learned from the experience. One of my favorite memories of this assignment involved a huge football player. He was a really tough jock who spent time with the kids with Down syndrome. During that time period, he joined them on a field trip. I still have a photograph from that trip. Right there in the middle, the football player is standing with about six kids hanging off him. They loved him and he loved them as well.

It is always important to realize that there may be something else going on in the student's brain besides what is going on in your class.

Chapter 7

Reaching Your Students

"Don't try to fix the students, fix ourselves first. The good teacher makes the poor student good and the good student superior. When our students fail, we too, as teachers, have failed."

— *Marva Collins, American educator (1936-Present)*

Teenagers may not be adults yet, but they are very astute. Regardless of their academic abilities, students will be able to sense your confidence level, or lack thereof. You have undoubtedly heard the expression, "never let them see you sweat." This is especially applicable to high school teachers. If teenagers believe that you are vulnerable, they may consider you weak and lose respect for you. In other words, even the kindest students will take every advantage they can to get what they want and to see you suffer, if you let them.

Introducing Yourself

First impressions are the most important ones, so strike quickly and effectively. Teenagers are a tough crowd, so plan accordingly. Consider the following when planning how you will introduce yourself to your new high school class.

- Get the students' attention
- Provoke interest and intrigue for you and the course

- Prove yourself worthy
- Gain their respect

The following are some suggested steps to take when planning your introduction:

1. Before you begin, make some notes about what you want to include.

2. List interesting and appropriate facts about yourself. Include your education, travel experience, and related interests. For example, your math students might not care if you own six cats. If you are a physical education teacher and you once played baseball for the New York Yankees, then that is a relevant fact that will interest your students.

3. Use a sense of humor — if you have one. Face it — not everyone is funny. If you are not normally known for your wit, do not under any circumstances try to fake it. You will end up being laughed at, but it will be behind your back.

4. Mention highlights of the course. You do not need to drone on about every book you will read, but you may want to mention planned field trips, plays, or interesting projects that are planned for the year.

5. Get the students immediately involved. Chances are, unless you start in the middle of the year, most of them are still lamenting the end of summer vacation. Discuss interesting current events from the summer that may pertain to the course material.

6. Use interesting visual aids to get their attention. However, they probably do not want to watch endless slides of your trip to see the world's ruins. In fact, if you turn the lights out, they will probably fall asleep or text-message each other on their cell phones under the desks. Instead, show them unusual props you brought back from a trip.

7. If the class is late in the day, you will have to work harder. Teenagers will be extremely sluggish from the mid day until about five minutes before the bell rings. Consider waking them up with music. Be sure it is appropriate, pertains to the class in some way, and does not disturb neighboring classes.

8. If you plan to use visual aids in your introduction, make sure they are contemporary but appropriate. Your students will become more engaged by viewing a YouTube (**www.YouTube.com**) video than they will be by something shown on a slide projector.

9. Consider using a costume element. For example, if you teach a foreign language, don a hat from that culture. If you teach Shakespeare, consider wearing a period piece to grab your students' attention.

10. If you are extremely nervous and do not have any idea how to introduce yourself in an entertaining way, consider a brief introduction, followed by an ice-breaking activity. That will take the attention away from you long enough for you to calm down and gain your composure. Consider using a game that involves all of the students, such as a game that will help you get to know more about their names and personalities. They may act like they think it is "lame," but if it gets them moving, keeps them awake, and has them laughing, you have succeeded.

Tricks to memorize names

Being able to remember names correctly is an asset in any business, and teaching is no exception. It may not seem like much to teachers, but incorrectly pronouncing or spelling a student's name can cause resentment. Memorizing your students' names is one of the most important tasks that you as a teacher will have to master. Being able to call your students by name is the first step in getting to know them, create a relationship with them, and gain their respect, which helps you in maintaining control of your classroom. If you cannot memorize your students' names, they will view you as an insensitive and uncaring adult.

One way to begin this process of learning your students' names and their proper spellings is to review their records. While you look over the folder of each student, write his or her first and last name, then jot down notes beside each of his or her name. This will help you remember specifics for each student and therefore help you remember their names.

There are a number of other tips for helping you to remember your students' names. Here are a few suggestions:

- Make a seating chart and have students sit in assigned seats for several weeks until you can associate names with faces.
- When you read forms from your students, mentally picture each face with the information you are reading.'
- Use association as you start to get to know the students. Use a word or phrase to help you remember names.
- Walk around the room while students are working, checking the roll with each pupil.
- On the first day of school, have each student say his or her name and repeat it.
- Repeat student names each time you talk to them. This will help cement it in your memory.
- Note pronunciation remarks on your roster and mark notes about characteristics for each student.
- If you forget a student's name, admit it, and then ask for help. When the student says his or her name, repeat it, write it down, and say it again.

Watching your students interact with one another is a great way to get to know them. Helping them get to know one another is another way to learn about your students and also helps them learn to value one another.

"Always try to call a student by his or her name. Get to know the names as soon as possible. This is a good idea for the other people you interact with as well. This is one of those tips from Dale Carnegie's book, *How to Win Friends and Influence People.* That book is my Bible; I've read it ten times. It is the best. I would recommend the book to anyone and everyone."

— Kathy Heisler, veteran teacher,
Cumberland Valley High School

Earning Their Respect

Most teenagers do not need you to be their friends. They need you to educate and inspire them to become responsible adults. They need guidance and discipline. They also need to know that you know more than they do, whether it be through acquired knowledge or life experience. That being said, teenagers do need to know that they matter. Some come from broken homes and bad circumstances. If you show them respect and let them know you care what they think and how they are feeling, they will reciprocate.

In a new environment, you need to introduce yourself. Plan what you want to relay to the individuals you will be working with all year. Teenagers have keen senses. They will be very aware of your appearance, how you smell, the tone of your voice, and your overall knowledge and confidence level.

1. **Appearance.** Dress appropriately and professionally. If you are young, be careful not to dress like your students — you do not want to be mistaken for a student. Dressing too casually or trendy can undermine your respectability. You can be fashionable, but dress conservatively. Make sure you are covered. Do not wear too much jewelry. Additionally, be it right or wrong, people are judged

first by their appearances. You may have a doctorate degree, but if you walk into a classroom of students and you have tattoos, unusual body piercings, or tight clothing that shows skin when you bend over, you will gain their attention for all the wrong reasons.

2. **Body language.** Students will react to other non-verbal clues as well. How you stand and the facial expressions you use will alert them to how you are feeling about them and the situation. They are very astute. They will be able to sense hostility, apathy, indifference, nervousness, and fear. Work on keeping your emotions in check and minimizing outward clues to any insecurity you may have.

3. **Smell.** This is a factor that applies to positive and negative scents. Obviously you will have issues with students if you have any body odor issues. This includes, but is not limited to, problems brought on by failing deodorant and bad breathe. Undoubtedly, you will need to deal with students who suffer from these issues as well. Plan to appropriately handle your own issues. In addition to remaining clean, keep extra deodorant and breathe mints in your desk for emergencies. Avoid things like eating onions and garlic at lunch and do not exercise in the middle of the day unless you have time to shower.

4. **Tone of voice.** Obviously your voice is yours to some extent. You can, however, control your tone and pitch. Practice with a tape recorder. Do not be too loud or too soft. Do not exhibit excitability, stress, signs of temper, or uncertainty when you speak. The students will notice these verbal clues and they will react to you accordingly.

5. **Knowledge and experience.** Prove your worth by commenting on experiences you have had that pertain to the lessons at hand. This is a subtle reminder that you do know what you are talking about and that you do have valid life experience that is interest-

ing, making you worth listening to. You do not need to share the specifics of your personal views on politics, religion, sports, pop culture, and other news, but it important to stay informed. If a student mentions something that is going on in the world and you have no idea what he is talking about, you will quickly lose credibility. It does not matter if it is relevant to the course you teach. You are dealing with burgeoning adults. If they think they know more than you, not only will you lose their respect, they will attempt to make you look unintelligent in front of the other students.

6. **Skills.** The average American teenager is very tech-savvy. A lack of understanding concerning computers, the Internet, cell phones, and any of the technological equipment in the classroom with lose you points very quickly. Students will feel superior and quite possibly shut out anything else you have to say. If you are not up to speed on the latest technology, find a young person who is not one of your students and have them help you get up to speed. Even if you do not use the following, it will help to know a little about them, so you understand what your students are talking about:

    - Facebook and MySpace
    - Twitter
    - E-mail, texting, and instant messaging
    - iPods and other MP3 players
    - Cell phones and smartphones
    - Laptops, netbooks, and other computers.
    - Game consoles, such as Microsoft Xbox, Sony PlayStation, Nintendo DS, and the Nintendo Wii

CASE STUDY: EARNING OUR RESPECT

Alexander Wise
Student
Trinity High School
Camp Hill, PA

Alex Wise is a junior at Trinity High School during the 2009 through 2010 school year. He and a number of his peers compiled a list of hints to help new incoming high school teachers.

My friends and I discuss teachers all of the time. Sometimes it is in a positive way, but many times we are talking about the things that bother us. In talking to a bunch of kids at my school, we came up with a list of ideas to help teachers. This is our perspective. Changing a few simple things can gain you a lot more respect.

1) Be yourself, particularly when it comes to humor. Don't try to be funny; just let it come naturally. I have a teacher who says, "high larious" as opposed to "hilarious," and nobody finds it funny. On the other hand, if connecting with students by way of making jokes is something that comes naturally to you, don't hold back. Students love a teacher who is funny without forcing it.

2) Students see you more as a teacher than as a friend. I have one teacher who will come up and talk like he's still in school. For example, he will say things like, "What's goin' on, man?" or "How's it hangin'?" These aren't things students are used to hearing, particularly from adults.

3) First impressions are key. Students always seem to form immediate impressions. I would say that it's good to smile and be welcoming, but not to the point where it becomes annoying. Also, no student wants to walk into a classroom on the first day of school to a teacher who looks more like a police officer.

4) As weird as it may sound, don't be creepy. As bad as it may sound, a male teacher of mine seems to hit on some of the girls in the class. As a result, students dislike him very much.

5) One thing a new teacher should do differently is to simply relax. First-year teachers, in my experience, tend to be nervous to the point where it actually affects their ability to teach. Though high school students can be intimidating, push through.

6) Also, new teachers should know that there will always be at least one troublemaker in every class. This is the student who never pays attention, always talks, and so forth. Sometimes, the best thing to do is simply ignore them and keep on teaching. Don't let them throw you off track, because that's exactly what they want.

The Issue of Sex

As a secondary teacher, you will encounter more issues involving sex than in other teaching positions. The problems range from addressing student public displays of affection to sexual harassment. Difficulties arising from raging hormones and teenage promiscuity run rampant in many high schools. As a new teacher, you must first determine the school's policies. Most schools have policies involving dress code, public displays of affection, and a code of conduct regarding student teacher interactions. Be sure you understand and follow the schools policies right from the beginning.

As a new young teacher, your friendliness or easy-going manner may be misinterpreted by a lonely student looking for attention. Here are a few basic precautions to follow:

- Make sure you are never alone with a student behind a closed door.
- Do not have a relationship with a student that involves texting, emailing, or social networking.
- Be wary of physical conduct, such as hugging. It may seem innocent, but it could also be misconstrued by the student or by others.

- Avoid using nicknames, such as "honey," sweetie," "cutie," or anything that may accidentally convey an inappropriate familiarity.

"My best advice for a new high school teacher just starting out is to do your best to be a role model and someone they can come to for help - not a friend. Too many teachers try to become friends with their students in order to gain respect and end up losing it because the students can't look at them as an adult or authority figure."

— Jen Mulhollen, itinerant learning support teacher, Cumberland Valley School District

The Mix of Students

No matter where you end up teaching, not all of your students will be the same. In some school districts, there is a lack of diversity and the majority of students may look similar on the outside. Regardless, each student is different. They each have their own hopes and fears. They each have their own learning styles and their own distinct feelings about school. Some will be positive and some will be negative, and you may not be able to tell how they really feel until you get to know them. Teenagers will do whatever they can to hide their true feeling and blend in with their peers. Although you may have been given some information that pertains to students' past performance, you will not be able to ascertain the reasons for the performance just by reading a file. The following are some of the factors that can affect high school students in their outward classroom behavior and achievement levels.

All students learn and perform differently. Traditionally, there are stereotypes for different types of students. For example, you may find yourself labeling certain students as jocks, geeks, cheerleaders, drama queens, troublemakers, or class clowns. If you do this, do not be too hard on yourself. We have been bombarded with stereotypes in books and movies. But the truth is that most students and adults have little bits of each of these characteristics inside of them. It is their individual circumstances that cause one or more of these elements to become more pronounced. When you find yourself relying on labels, consider the end of the letter from The Breakfast Club, written by Anthony Michael Hall's character:

> *"We accept the fact that we had to sacrifice a whole Saturday in detention for whatever it was we did wrong. But we think you're crazy to make us write an essay telling you who we think we are. You see us as you want to see us — in the simplest terms, in the most convenient definitions. But what we found out is that each one of us is a brain, and an athlete, and a basket case, a princess, and a criminal. Does that answer your question?"*

That being said, you will have to deal with a full spectrum of capabilities. Some students will be gifted and others will be challenged. Most will be somewhere in between. The interesting part comes in discovering those who are not necessarily obvious. For example, writing good lesson plans will include adaptations for all ends of the spectrum. You may think you know who the gifted and challenged individuals are. The truth may actually surprise you. Many high school students do not relay their abilities in front of their peers and are actually working either below, or in some cases, above their abilities.

Intelligence Quotient (IQ) is not the only factor that determines student performance. Many other issues affect achievement abilities as well. For example:

- **Socio-economic issues.** This covers a number of matters. Some students may have more or less support and or advantages than other students. Teenagers are very susceptible to peer pressure and may react accordingly.

- **Problems at home.** Teenagers do not always want to discuss their problems. They may have added pressures from a difficult home life. Money issues, alcoholism, abuse, and divorce are just a few of the topics that may plague your students.

- **Health problems.** Feeling well is definitely an advantage when it comes to completing your work and paying attention. Health-related issues encompass many areas. Prolonged colds, sleep deprivation, lack of adequate nutrition, visual disturbances, disability, chronic medical conditions, and multiple absences from illnesses all can affect student performance.

CASE STUDY: HOW TEACHERS CAN HELP STUDENTS WITH CHRONIC HEALTH PROBLEMS

Susan Minnich
Care Coordinator
Penn State Hershey
Children's Hospital
(800) 243-1455

Susan Minnich is the Care Coordinator for the Children's Hospital at Penn State Hershey Medical Center. She serves as a patient advocate and helps chronically sick children transition back into their regular routines when they leave the hospital. One of the areas she coordinates is school communication. This case study discusses the issue of maintaining a student's education under difficult circumstances involving a medical diagnosis.

My responsibilities include assisting medically fragile children. This information is intended to provide teachers with some background information and advice on handling situations involving these types of students.

Discharging medically fragile children to home from the hospital requires coordination of services. Sending these same children to school is a challenge. From age 5 to graduation, a child's main goal is to complete their education. Most children struggle with this at some point in time. Children who have a chronic medical condition have an added dimension that can complicate an easy schedule or make a heavy schedule seem impossible. Returning to school does not have to be that difficult. The issues that can complicate returning to school differ at each level.

Teenagers are a challenge when they are well; add a chronic diagnosis, new or old, and you really have your hands full. Teenagers with chronic diseases are known for their poor compliance. They do not want to be different, they do not want to be reliant on medication, and they are rebellious. At this age, they need to know about their disease and the treatment. They should be taking on the responsibility of their own care. Usually they know it all, just choose not to act. Again, not drawing attention to these students is the first priority. For example, Crohn's disease is an inflammatory bowel condition that creates extreme discomfort for those affected. Teens with Crohn's disease have little time to wait when they have to use the restroom. These students should not have to ask permission to have a restroom break. They should be able to go as needed without drawing attention to themselves.

Over the years, I have encountered many different scenarios. Here are few suggestions for dealing with medically fragile students:

1. If possible, learn about the disease that your student has. It may help you understand a lot more about the individual as well.

2. Ask the parents questions when you can. If that isn't possible, talk the school nurse. It is important to know what signs to look for to determine whether the student needs help.

3. Try to minimize the attention that you draw to that student — both good and bad. More often than not, the individual does not want to have the extra attention, especially if it concerns their condition.

4. Be respectful of their right to privacy. If they want to talk about the condition, they will. If they do not want to talk about it, let it go. Being different in any way is difficult for a child. If the issue includes pain or other difficulties, it becomes even more of a challenge.

5. Despite needing to understand and perhaps even watch for signs of trouble, it is important to treat these students like everyone else.

Encountering Students with Non-Academic Problems

There are elements in place to provide assistance to students who need something additional in respect to academics. These individualized plans help gifted students and students who struggle with learning disabilities and chronic medical conditions. Unfortunately, there are many other students who struggle for completely unrelated reasons. In addition to doing their schoolwork, many teenagers have other very major issues in their lives to contend with. Some may come from broken homes. Others may have to work full-time hours to help pay the family's bills. Consider these facts when interacting with students who may appear to be difficult. The following is a list of just a few potential issues facing teens and their family members today:

- Bullying
- Drugs/alcohol
- Depression
- Isolation
- Sex and pregnancy
- Anorexia/bulimia
- Low self-esteem
- Thoughts of suicide
- Problems at home
- Physical and/or mental abuse
- Poverty
- Gang violence
- Divorce

Negativity, a lack of respect for authority figures, anger, sadness, and a total absence of joy are potential warning signs. Since the school violence tragedies of Columbine and Virginia Tech, schools have been more aware of issues concerning potentially troubled students. However, it is important to avoid inappropriately labeling individual students because they appear to have early warning signs of being troubled. Pay attention to what you see and discuss it with a counselor at the school. It is important to pay attention, but it is just as critical that you not jump to conclusions. Here are some of the warning signs as identified by high school and university counselors all over the country:

- Exhibits antisocial behaviors or indications of loneliness.
- Shows no close bonds or friendships with other students.
- Frequently expresses an extremist viewpoint.
- Idolizes inappropriate figures, such as serial killers or Satan.
- Depicts sense of hopelessness and despair suddenly for no known cause.
- Displays an unexplainable preoccupation with weapons.
- Caught for carrying some form of weapon.
- Appears to have little, if any, supervision by parent or guardian.
- Appear to have witnessed or experienced an abusive home life.
- Expressed suicidal thoughts.
- Has threatened or attempted suicide.
- Demonstrated self-mutilating, such as cutting or burning of his or herself.
- Made and or carried out threats to others.
- Exhibits intimidating behaviors, such as invading personal space, inappropriate touching, unnecessary roughness, harassment, or stalking.
- Previously experienced bullying, harassment, and torment from peers.
- Frequently bullies or intimidates those who are younger or weaker.
- Openly exhibits violent behavior.
- Expresses or brags of future plans of violence.

- Exhibits difficulty in controlling his anger and other extreme emotions.
- Exhibits constant signs of nervousness and tension.
- Cries often for inexplicable reasons.
- Displays consistent signs of clinical depression or has noticeable mood swings.
- Displays sudden decline in work habits, such as excessive procrastination and decreased quality of prepared work.
- Frequently misses school and makes no effort to get caught up on missed work.
- Exhibits signs of dependency on adults by hanging around excessively.
- Display frequent signs of listlessness and lethargy, frequently falling asleep in class.
- Marked decline in personal hygiene
- Report of physical assault or recent loss of someone important, such as friend or family member.
- Displays signs of low self-esteem
- Frequently blames others or refuses to take responsibility for his or her own actions.
- Displays an inability to be sympathetic toward others.
- Prefers violent media (violent TV shows, movies, and computer games) to all else.
- Repeatedly uses themes of violence or hatred in writings and artwork.
- Has a history of disciplinary problems.
- Has a history of substance abuse.
- Expresses feelings of intolerance or prejudice.

- Exhibits feelings of superiority.
- Openly discusses an interest in or an involvement in gangs.
- Displays a blatant disregard for rules and regulations, as if they do not pertain to him or her.
- Exhibits difficulty in coping with a significant life change or failure.
- Exhibits cruelty to animals.

If you encounter students who may be troubled or difficult, there are a number of approaches you can try:

1. Try talking to the student. Sometimes the individual merely needs someone to talk to. Once you ascertain the problem, you can decide how to obtain assistance if it is necessary. Do not promise confidentiality. If a student poses a threat to themselves or someone else at school, someone needs to be notified.

2. Talk to the school counselor or school psychologist. If you believe the issue is beyond your comfort level or requires assistance outside of the school, do not hesitate to ask for help. For example, if there is a concern about violence or criminal activity, it may demand law enforcement. If the situation is more personal in nature, such as pregnancy, depression, or substance abuse, you may need to involve a physician or psychiatrist. There are suicide hotlines and groups for teens living with substance abuse in the family, and school counselors have extensive resources on issues pertaining to troubled teens.

3. Talk to the student's parent or guardian. If you notice a marked change in behavior that is inexplicable, there may be cause concern. On the other hand, it may be simply a bad time because of a family member's illness or loss of a job. Before approaching the parent or guardian, speak with the school counselor or an administrator about school protocol unless you have already developed a report with the parent or guardian.

Bullying

Schools can no longer ignore bullying situations. As we are seeing with increasing frequency in the news, bullying can have serious consequences. For example, in March 2010, nine Massachusetts teens faced police charges for bullying a 15-year-old girl on Facebook for several weeks, leading up to her suicide. The case culminated in new anti-bullying legislation in the state senate and house.

Veteran language arts teacher Penny Martin believes the way to deal with bullying among students is to change the attitude of bullies and recipients. She says, "Bullying is a problem wherever there are living beings. It occurs not only in classrooms, but also in families, workplaces, communities, and the interaction of states and nations. Some would say that it is forever part of the natural world, and others would even say that it serves to build strength in those who survive it." She believes that to deal with bullying, you must "recognize it, understand it, and remold the attitudes of both bully and recipient." This three-step approach is a great way for you to prevent and deter bullying problems with your students.

Recognizing bullying

There are multiple types of bullies, Dan Olweus, author of *Bullying at School: What We Know and What We Can Do,* defines a victim of bullying as someone who is "exposed, repeatedly and over time, to negative actions on the part of one or more other persons, and he or she has difficulty defending himself or herself." He details more specifically the characteristics of bullying as follows:

- Aggressive behavior that involves unwanted, negative actions
- A pattern of behavior repeated over time
- An imbalance of power or strength

This definition will manifest itself in many ways, from your classroom all the way to the cafeteria. Be aware of the indications. Here are some of the specifics that can help you recognize when bullying is occurring:

- **Verbal abuse:** Although you can observe many types of bullying throughout middle school hallways and classrooms, verbal abuse is a more common behavior among adolescents. It includes derogatory comments about the victim or the victim's family or friends, name-calling, and put-downs such as "stupid." Crass or sarcastic remarks veiled as supposedly humorous puns count. In that case, you may find the victim laughing along with the bully or others, but deep down it is a hurtful remark that scars.

- **Deliberate isolation:** This is not particular to groups of adolescent girls, but it is a phenomenon more often found among them and often with individuals who were once friends. Students often ostracize another with cruel intent, perhaps excluding the victim from the lunch table, deliberately leaving the victim for last when choosing partners or teams, or setting him or her apart through deliberate lies and false rumors.

- **Physical abuse:** Whether to extort money from another student or simply to pick on someone for kicks, shoving in the halls, hitting, kicking, and spitting is most certainly bullying. It is not necessarily the most common form, but it is certainly the most recognizable form.

- **Sexual harassment:** If children have not learned appropriate forms of touch, they need to know now. This goes for bullies and their victims. A slap on the butt is inappropriate and no joke, despite what bullies and possibly the victims who laugh it off may think.

- **Cyber bullying (via texting or the Internet):** StopCyberbullying.org (**www.stopcyberbullying.org**), an excellent Web site for learning about, preventing, and thwarting cyber bullying, defines it as "when a child, preteen, or teen is tormented, threatened, harassed, humiliated, embarrassed, or otherwise targeted by another child, preteen, or teen using the Internet, interactive and digital technologies, or mobile phones. It has to have a minor on both sides, or at least have been instigated by a minor against another minor."

- **Racism and prejudice:** Bullies can use any of the above strategies to torment someone because of race, religion, sexual preference, size, or peer group. If not redirected in adolescence, this type of bullying can turn into a community issue that no one, except those who are ignorant of its ability to destroy, wants.

Understanding bullying

Dr. Marlene Snyder's online article "Understanding Bullying and Its Impact on Kids With Learning Disabilities or AD/HD" said bullies are not who we once thought they were: students with low self-esteem. "Bullies, in fact, may be average students or even classroom or athletic leaders," she says. Snyder said it is the victims who usually suffer from low self-esteem and view themselves negatively. They often consider themselves failures and feel stupid, ashamed, and unattractive. "They may come to believe that they 'deserve' to be bullied. They are often lonely, friendless, and abandoned at school," she said. These traits also may mean empowering victims is part of the prevention equation. Olweus offers a better understanding of how to do this by describing two types of victims:

The Passive victim

- Is non assertive and through his actions may signal to others that he or she is insecure and will not retaliate if attacked or insulted
- Is cautious, quiet, or anxious
- Cries easily and collapses quickly when bullied
- Has few friends and is not connected to a social network
- Lacks humor and pro-social skills
- May be physically weak

The Provocative victim

- Is both anxious and aggressive

- May cause irritation and disruption around him or her
- Is easily emotionally aroused
- Prolongs the conflict even when losing

Redirecting attitudes

Given Olweus' and Snyder's research on this subject, regardless of whether the victims or the bullies are the ones with low-self-esteem issues, it is important to empower students to value themselves and others. Here are a few suggestions:

- Begin with prevention by teaching tolerance: a zero-tolerance policy for bullying in and out of the classroom and 100 percent tolerance for diversity in our classrooms, homes, and communities. For ideas, explore the Teaching Tolerance Web site, **www.teachingtolerance.com**. Much of what the site offers is free, and you can even sign up to receive a complimentary quarterly magazine with articles and ideas on teaching tolerance.

- When using group work or pairs in your lesson plans, be sure to choose the groups, especially if you suspect there is a problem. Additionally, it is best if students have an opportunity to work with different individuals instead of always being with the same group or partners.

- Immediately report any talk of bullying, including threatening notes, to the assistant principal, or the person in charge of discipline.

- Any time you become aware of any type of weapon, let someone in authority know. It may help avert a serious tragedy.

Working with teenagers is a challenge. In some ways, they seem like adults, and at others they seem very immature. They are trying to find their place in the world — a world that is also full of challenges. Realizing all of the issues that confront teenagers daily can seem overwhelming. Be patient, respectful, and sympathetic to what they are going through. John Sculley, former CEO of

PepsiCo and Apple stated it best when he said, "We expect teachers to handle teenage pregnancy, substance abuse, and the failings of the family. Then we expect them to educate our children."

Chapter 8

Working With Parents and Guardians

"The problem with children is that you have to put up with their parents."

— Charles de Lint, Canadian author (1951-Present)

When children go to elementary school, there are numerous opportunities for teacher and parent interactions. There are scheduled conferences, classrooms visits, and multiple parties and social gatherings for parents to attend. Additionally, more people are likely to be at home with younger children. As they get older, things change. Parents who may have stayed out of the workforce temporarily often return to work. Older students also have multiple teachers instead of one and written communication that is sent home with the student may or may not ever be seen by the parents.

As children progress into adolescence, parent and children relationships become strained. As a result, teenagers are much less likely to communicate with their parents about what is happening at school. Add that to the fact that there are more complicated issues facing these teenagers, and you end up with a scary combination for most parents. Now, more than ever, communication concerning the students is critical. There are a number of issues that require communication between teachers and parents. Here is a generalized list of some of the issues that may constitute communication with a parent or guardian:

- Academic concerns
- Medical concerns

- Behavioral concerns
- School policy issues
- Parental involvement request

Effective Teacher/Parent Communication

In school you spent a lot of you time in your courses discussing child development issues, teaching practices, and educational trends. This information prepares you to teach. Student interaction may be different than learning in a classroom, but for the most part, you are relatively prepared after you complete your student teaching internship. Nothing, however, prepares you for the part of the job that involves you dealing with the parents and guardians of your students.

Just as your students are all different and unique, so are their parents. Some school districts will be more diverse than others, evoking additional challenges. Regardless, there will be many differences in the guardians. Stop to consider some of the obvious variables. Some of these include:

- **Age** — Some parents and guardians will be very young while others may be older.
- **Background** — Some may be highly educated, others may have little or no formal education.
- **Parental Status** — Actual married parents, single divorced parents, and many types of other legal guardians.
- **Socio-economic background and standing** — A variety in how they grew up and how they live now.
- **Cultural diversity** — Multiple nationalities, races, and religions.

It is challenging to teach a diverse group of individuals, but it can be even more challenging to communicate with their parents. With students, you are dealing with individuals of the same age and generational mindset who probably live in relatively similar areas. There are many more variables in their parents and guardians. In addition to the factors mentioned, there are also personality differences. In other words, some parents will be more excited about their child's education than others. Here are a few examples of the types of parents or guardians you may encounter:

- **Over-achiever** — Recognizes abilities in child and feels very competitive. Expects the best out their child and wants to ensure that you will to.
- **Worrier** — Needs constant assurances that their child is doing fine.
- **Enabler** — May be overly involved in students work and always seek ways for you to cut the student a break.
- **Apathetic** — Does not have any concerns, does not respond to your attempts at communication, or believes high school is just something you have to get through.
- **Defender** — Assumes the worst and automatically gets defensive when you approach them.
- **Accuser** — Blames you for not doing a good enough job with the student.

There will be times when it is very difficult to communicate effectively with the adults in your student's life. Accept that now and you will save yourself a lot of anguish. Breathe deeply and do the best you can to try to communicate effectively. Here are some tips to help you along the way.

- At the beginning of the school year gather contact information on all of your students. Keep it somewhere you can access it as needed.

- Open the lines of communication. Introduce yourself to the guardians and let them know how they can contact you if they have any concerns. You can do this in a letter and at back-to-school night. Realize that even with your best intentions, everyone probably will not see it or read it, but at least you have made an attempt.

- Clarify expectations. This is important for the students and parents. You can write it in a document, put it on your Web site, post it in your classroom, and state it in person.

- Document everything. In order to protect yourself, document all forms of communication with the students and their guardians. If there is e-mail correspondence, print it off and save it in a file. If you speak on the phone, make notes and keep them in the file. If anything goes home, get a signed copy for the file. If it does not get returned, document that as well.

- Know the school policies for handling disputes with parents and guardians.

- Use discretion and practice confidentiality.

- Avoid criticizing. Offer feedback and suggestions and try to remain positive.

- Depending on the type of school, the surrounding community, and the district size, you may or may not have much interaction with the parents and guardians of your students. For example, if you teach at a small Catholic high school that encourages a great deal of parent involvement, you may get to know many of the parents. On the other hand, if you teach in an urban area, or a very large public school, you may only have occasional brief interaction with guardians. These are the primary situations that would involve teacher parent interaction:

- Back-to-school night
- Conference
- School-sanctioned event, such as a play, sporting event, or academic competition

Back-to-School Night (BTS)

As a high school teacher, you will be expected to participate in an evening event for parents and guardians. In some areas of the country, it is called back-to-school night; in others it is called open house. Generally, it is held at least a month or so into the school year. This gives you some time to get to know all of your students. If you teach multiple classes, it still may be a challenge, but do your best to at least be able to identify everyone by name by that point. Depending on your school, Back-to-School Night may or may not be a well-attended event. Here are some strategies for making the most out of the event:

- Make sure you can pronounce students names (first and last) accurately.

- Remember that students' and parents' last names are not necessarily the same. It may be a situation of divorce or guardianship. If you did not have the students fill out contact information for you on the first day, have them provide you this information before BTS. Adults will appreciate your efforts with this attention to detail.

- Ask your students for a head count on who plans to attend BTS. It may not be 100 percent accurate, but it will give you a general idea who you will be meeting.

- BTS tends to make for a long day. Most teachers find that there is not enough time to go home between school and BTS. Plan accordingly. Bring a change of clothes and anything else you might need to freshen up, such as a toothbrush, hairbrush, and deodorant.

- Try to take time to clear your head. If possibly, take a walk outside to get some fresh air and think about the evening ahead.

- Make sure you are in your room and ready to go at least 30 minutes before the event begins. Some people will be early and will not be thrilled if they have to wait in the hall.

- Pack an extra meal or snacks. It is a marathon day. Do not let your energy fall because of hunger and thirst.

- Prepare the classroom. In addition to straightening the desks and chairs used by the students, locate extra chairs to place in the room in case the attendance surpasses your class size.

- Make sure the room is clean and free from unnecessary clutter.

- Prepare your presentation. Since high school students have a different teacher for each subject, the parents will not be in your room long. The school will have an abbreviated schedule, so the attendees can visit each class. It is unlikely that you will have more than 15 to 20 minutes to talk.

- Have extra copies of your syllabus on hand. Since you are dealing with high school students, it is likely that most of the people in the room do not know any specifics about what you are teaching. Discuss your expectations of the students, what kinds of projects and papers they will be doing, and how you plan to assess them.

- Since time is limited, pass out papers to the attendees and ask them to please listen, rather than ask questions, unless there is time at the end. Ask the parents to write down their questions with their name and contact information. Collect the papers as they leave the room. This allows you time to formulate your answers prior to contacting them. It also alleviates being put on the spot.

- Provide parents with an acceptable means of contacting you. Give them an e-mail address or school phone number. Be cautious about giving out personal e-mail addresses and phone numbers. Some parents may take advantage of this information.

- Place a sign-in sheet by the door. It will be helpful to know who attended and in the quick pace of the evening, you may not get to meet everyone individually. This is also a good time to have them sign up for conference times, if you plan to have them.

- Finally, plan to linger for a specific amount of time, in case anyone has pressing concerns. Be sure to state what that amount of time is and stick to it; otherwise you could get stuck for hours. Plan an appropriate amount of time, such as 30 to 40 minutes. When that pre-set time is up, politely excuse yourself saying you need to get home. Offer another means of contact at another time if necessary, or have them set up a conference.

The Conference

On the subject of conferences, talk to other teachers at your school and find out what they generally do. Some high schools do not have conferences for every student. They save them for need-based individuals, unless a parent or guardian specifically requests one. Some teachers hold e-mail or hold phone conferences. Video conferencing (through the free online program Skype, for example) may be another option depending on your school's technology. If you do schedule conferences, consider the topics you will cover and have samples of the students work available for reference.

Academics

Parents and guardians generally want to be kept apprised of their children's progress. In the instances where there is not someone to communicate with, ask the guidance counselor for suggestions. In the earlier grades, graded assignments or notices from the school are sent home with students almost every day. It is relatively easy for parents to keep up with what is going on at school. As children age, it gets progressively more difficult. Teenagers may receive papers with grades on them and notes to take home, but more often than not, parents and guardians will never see them. There are a number of potential causes for the disparity:

- Statistically, more parents work outside of the home when the children are older.
- Technically, older children can handle their own workload and involve parents less.
- Teenagers develop autonomy and do not go to their parents for every issue in their life on a daily basis.
- Teenagers may be preoccupied with sports, jobs, or love interests.

Whatever the reason, parents are not always aware of everything going on with their teenage children, particularly when it comes to school. Some teachers try to solve this problem by requiring parent signatures on work and negative interim progress reports. This may work with some students. Others will conveniently "lose" the papers or quite possibly even forge their guardian's signature. Some schools mail the reports to the house rather than send it with the student. Again that may, or may not, be effective if the student gets home before their parents. So what should you, as the teacher, do? Pay attention. If you think the potential exists that a parent or guardian may not have seen something you wanted them to see, follow up with an e-mail or phone call.

CASE STUDY: COMMUNICATING WITH PARENTS

Douglas Wise
High School Parent
New Cumberland, PA

Douglas Wise is the father of two children. His oldest son is 17 years old and a junior at Trinity Catholic High School. He offers his thoughts on effective parent-teacher communication.

How do you prefer to be contacted by a teacher?

If the communication is factual in nature and merely informative, not requiring feedback or response, e-mail is fine. Otherwise, a phone call would be the preferred method, in my opinion. If the contact involves any form of discussion of facts or perspective, or the communication needs to be timely, I would definitely prefer a phone call.

About what types of situations do you believe teachers should notify parents?

There are a number of things I would like to hear about, both positive and negative. If there are any events or occurrences (academic excellence or witnesses of Christian fellowship) that are either above or below the norm, I would like to be informed. Likewise, if there are particular ongoing behavioral issues or sustained events that walk the line between acceptable and unacceptable behavior, I believe I should be notified.

Do you expect to meet with each of your child's high school teachers?

Yes. I expect to meet all of my son's teachers at least once during an orientation session at the beginning of each school year.

How often do you expect to meet with high school teachers?

I think meeting with each of the teachers at an orientation or back-to-school event is sufficient. The exception would be if an issue or other circumstance that warranted a face-to-face meeting or discussion.

What kinds of things do you want to discuss when you meet or speak with your child's teachers?

My primary expectation is to hear about my son's academic effort, and secondarily the academic results. I am also interested in hearing about his grasp of the subject matter and if it is the appropriate level. I want to know if it is too easy or too challenging. Finally, I want to know about the student's overall attitude and behavior in the classroom.

Can you provide at least one example of a positive and a negative regarding teacher communication?

The best, most effective communications in my experience have been sit-down, face-to-face discussions with teachers. I appreciate meetings that are structured to cover the points, but allow enough flexibility to answer issues pertinent to my child.

Many schoolteacher communications fail to answer the basic questions: who, what, when, where, why, and how. Additionally, I have found that many of these schoolteacher communications are untimely requiring a one- or two-day turnaround. That is not always possible for working and travelling parents. By far, the worst situation I ever encountered involved a teacher who lied in an e-mail to the parents. Upon being questioned about the untruth, the individual again lied to the parents and the student in a face-to-face meeting that included his direct supervisor. Nothing was done to rectify the situation. Lack of action in these types of circumstances tends to undermine parents' overall confidence in the school administration.

A solution for the future

Some schools have improved communication between parents and teachers with technology. These schools incorporate online grading systems that parents may access. The programs provide access to student assignments as well as posted grades for tests, quizzes, homework, and papers. This is very effective for parents who want to know what is going on with their children. They can access the information on a regular basis from their own computers at any time of day or night at their convenience. They also offer the ability to click on an e-mail link to contact the teacher with questions and concerns. School districts with technological capabilities have opted to institute these kinds of programs as a means to cut costs by going paperless.

One commonly used application by the Cumberland Vally School District in Mechanicsburg, Pennsylvania is called eSchoolBook. The program is set up by the school district and is maintained by the technology department. Teachers are expected to enter grades on a weekly basis unless otherwise specified, although parents and students can access them daily to see any updates. In these schools, technology is favored over paper reports. Teachers still have the ability to print hard copies of progress reports when the need arises. For example, if a student does not have a computer in the home, you still have the traditional options:

- Print off a copy to send home with the student
- Mail a hard copy of the report to the parent or guardian
- Call the parent or guardian and discuss your concerns

The eSchoolBook information is password protected so no one else can access you children's information. Currently, the program provides online for students in grades 6 through 12. Additionally, family members are linked, so parents can access all their children with one password. School districts generally require parents to attend a seminar explaining the program. Subsequently, they need to fill out an application and they must produce their driver's license to prove who they are. The application is reviewed before it is submitted to the technology department. This adds an element of safety. Teachers find it can be both a blessing and a curse.

Schools with available technology can close the communication gap between teachers and guardians. In addition to providing grades online, teachers at many schools have their own class-related Web sites. These sites include copies of the syllabus and information about the curriculum. They include calendars of upcoming homework, projects, and tests. Cumberland Valley High School in Mechanicsburg, Pennsylvania is an example of a technologically advanced school. They have a comprehensive school Web site that allows teachers and parents to communicate freely with each other as often as necessary. The school even posts the daily announcements. Of course, like anything else, it is only as effective as the individuals who take advantage of it. In today's busy times, as we become increasingly dependent on technology, it serves as a positive progressive step towards keeping the lines of communication open. To review eSchoolBook, go to the "Student Services" tab, followed by the "Technology" tab and click on "eSchoolBook" at **www.cvschools.org**.

As a new teacher, you may want to check the teacher's individual Web sites for the types of information that is provided in this public domain. Check to see if your school has the capacity for this type of program. If not, and you live in an area where most people are technologically advanced, you still can create your own Web site for parents to access. You will not be able to post grades, but you can provide a syllabus and calendar for their review. This is helpful if students have computers at home and are able to check assignments.

When the technology is not there

Given the push to improve schools across the country, schools without technology are slowly disappearing. That may improve some of your lesson plans, but it may not aid in parent teacher communication. A school may have computers for students, but that does not ensure that the students have access to technology at home. Many areas in the United States are severely impoverished. In these instances, communication may be more difficult. Here are some issues you may encounter with parents and guardians in this situation:

- Cultural diversity, differences in beliefs
- Language barriers
- Low socio-economic status
- Lack of education
- Higher level of stress
- Preoccupied single parent
- Substance abuse issues
- Violence in the home
- Lack of concern, lower perceived importance of school

How can you communicate effectively in these types of situations? It is considerably more difficult, but not always impossible. First and more most, you will have to be patient and persistent. In an effort to improve failing schools, some organizations offer special training for teachers willing to work in these areas. Here are some suggestions for effective communication under these circumstances:

- **Empathy** — Make a concerted effort to understand the different cultures and religions, without passing judgment.

- **Respect** — Show respect for the students and their families. Exhibit a belief that anyone can be successful and everyone deserves the same opportunity to learn.
- **Flexibility** — Be willing to adjust expectations as necessary.
- **Patience** — Cultural and language barriers may make communication challenging. Be patient and seek help from a counselor, translator, another teacher, or a student to understand what is being communicated.

The area of discipline

Over the years, thoughts on discipline in the classroom have changed. Research indicates that a positive proactive approach eliminates some of the negative behavior in the classroom. Teachers that incorporate the following have fewer problems in classroom management:

- High expectations for their students to achieve and succeed
- Classroom behavior expectations that are conveyed and enforced with the students
- Consistent daily routines that students understand
- A positive relationship with the class as a whole, not just a few individuals
- Positive feedback offered at regular intervals
- Consistent appropriate methods for identifying and handling misconduct
- A vehicle for relaying these expectations to both the students and their parents or guardians

One of the best ways to ensure positive results is to partner with parents and guardians from the beginning of the year. One way to do this is to provide a written statement of your expectations. The statement should include academics and behavior. Ask students to get it signed by a parent or guardian and return it to you. Include some way for parents and guardians to get in touch with you if they have concerns. By getting involved from the onset and keeping the door open for communication, you increase your chances for success. Additionally, if you have a Web site, post the expectations and your contact information for parents to review if necessary.

"It is beneficial to be disciplined at the beginning of the year with plenty of structure in your classroom, rather than the opposite way around. Avoid going into the beginning of the school year with a laid back attitude and little or no ground rules. Let students know what you expect of them the minute the bell rings. It is easier to ease up throughout the school year than to get tougher as the year goes by."

— Michael Lutz, world cultures teacher, Cumberland Valley High School

Despite being positive and prepared, some issues will still arise. Parents will generally be much more supportive of you and helpful in issues concerning the disciplining of their children if you contact them as soon as a problem arises. For example, if you see a sudden decline in the student's work ethic, it may be a red flag. If the student did their homework in the beginning of the year and suddenly stops turning items in and starts do poorly on tests and quizzes, it is appropriate to make contact with the parent. Most parents want to know before their child is so far behind that it becomes difficult to rectify the situation. In many cases, there may be a difficult situation creating stress for the student. For the best results, teachers and parents or guardians need to work together. If other issues exist, school counselors and nurses can be called in as needed. The key is keeping the lines of communication open.

Helpful hints for handling bad behavior and preventing it from becoming a bigger issue:

- First attempt to diffuse the situation with humor.
- Silence until they stop.
- Stare blatantly at the offender.
- Hover near the offending person(s).
- Remove the offender. Have him or her move to a different location in the room.
- Relocate the offender to the office.
- Give detention.
- Give a pop quiz.
- Threaten to involve coach or club adviser.

Forms of Communication and the Pros and Cons of Each

During the first 18 years of their lives, most American children spend about 85 percent of their time under the guidance and influence of their parents or guardians. If the environment includes positive adult involvement, the children have a better chance of a positive outcome later in life. There is no guarantee, but according to most studies, it helps. A study conducted by the George W. Bush administration in 2000 indicated that parents are a vital component of the academic future success of the student. A lack of parental involvement can be a major obstacle in the hope for school work improvement. Keep this in mind as you encounter different types of parents. Keeping the lines of communication open offers the best chance for a successful outcome for everyone involved.

"When your kids get to high school, everything changes. The kids don't tell you everything and they don't bring things home to show you anymore. They have multiple teachers and you have no idea what is going on until the reports cards come home. Some school districts have online grading, but ours does not. I think that would be very helpful. I would really appreciate hearing from the teachers if they think something is going on with my child. If there is a drop in grades or overall performance, or if their behavior changes, or worse yet if they notice something disturbing, I want to know about it. A student might not bring notes home; I think e-mails and phone calls are the best way to reach parents."

— Linda Weaver, parent, Mechanicsburg, PA

Notes

Notes to parents at the high school level are probably the least effective form of communication. If you send a note home with a teenager, the parent may or may not ever see it. If you mail the note to his or her house, it has a better chance of reaching the guardian, but this too is not guaranteed. Many students this age are at home alone long before their parents get home from work. If the teenager gets the mail, he or she may prevent the parents from ever seeing it. If you do send home a written note, ask for a signed reply from the parent or guardian indicating that they saw it. Do not take the word of the student. This too is not foolproof; many teenagers can forge their parents' signatures.

E-mail

With today's technology, many people communicate via e-mail. It is quick and efficient, particularly if you are lucky enough to have a computer in your classroom. If you do not, and school access is limited, you can do this from home or the library. If e-mail is a viable option for communicating with the student's guardian, it will be listed on their contact information. Not everyone has a work or home computer, so keep this is mind. Additionally, if an issue is time-sensitive, this is not the best option because not every checks their e-mail on a regular basis.

"If a parent e-mails you with a concern or an issue, do not go immediately blaming their child for the problems they are facing. Be understanding about parent concerns. If you feel strongly about an issue, then stand firm on it. When communicating via e-mail, always have a colleague check over your e-mail. They will offer you advice and make sure you have worded your comments delicately and appropriately."

— Michael Lutz, world cultures teacher, Cumberland Valley High School

Phone calls

The majority of parents interviewed for this book agreed that phone calls are the most effective form of communication, particularly when the issue is serious or time-sensitive. It is the only way you can be sure the message is relayed. For best results, send an e-mail or note to the parent or guardian letting them know you wish to speak with them. Ask if there is a good time you could contact them on the phone. If you do not get a response within two days, place a phone call to the guardian and leave a message.

In both written and oral communication, be professional and polite. Stay calm and simply state the issue. Also, be sure you relate your expectations. Do not place the burden of results on the parent. Make sure to let the individual know that you want to work as a team to help the student. Remember, the point is to approach the situation with a positive course of action. If you are judgmental and accusatory, you will most likely make the parent defensive. This will put unnecessary barrier between the two of you, making it more difficult to work together in the best interest of the student.

If you call and are unable to reach someone, continue to try until you reach the person you need to speak to. Keep track of the amount of times you tried to contact someone. Do not assume that a message has been relayed. The school keeps records of the students' guardians and their contact information. Check with the school secretaries to obtain phone numbers. The school nurse is another source. Most schools require emergency contact forms that the nurse keeps on file.

Any time you speak with a parent or guardian, you need to document the conversation. You may need to provide proof at some point that you did everything you could to assist the child under a specific set of circumstances. There are many ways to organize your documentation. Some teachers keep a communication log, and others write up individual notes and keep them in the student's file. Do what works for you. Just be sure to do it consistently in order to protect yourself.

Be prepared for resistance. When you need to call parents regarding an issue concerning their children, it is probably not going to make them happy. Some will handle better than others, but understand it is not any fun for you to make the call and it is not going to be fun to receive it either. Here are a few situations you may encounter:

1. **Denial.** This is when a parent is overtly dismissive of your suggestion or concern, saying things like, "My child would never…" The best way to handle the situation is to be quiet until the news sinks in. Let the parent absorb what you have just told him. Wait until he is done venting, and explain the entire situation calmly, stating only the facts. Do not pass judgment or allow your tone of voice to convey anything other than a factual recounting of the event of circumstance. Do not allow yourself to be baited. If you encounter yelling, or berating on the other end of the line, stay calm and say, "I am sorry you feel that way. I just needed to call you and inform you of the situation." Get off the phone and

document the conversation. If further action needs to occur, you can provide documentation of the first notification.

2. **Silence.** A parent in denial may get you upset. Despite that, a silent parent may be even more difficult to deal with, particularly since you are on the phone and cannot see her. You end up doing all of the talking and without seeing any facial expressions, you have no idea what she is thinking. Again, let the news sink in, make sure someone is still on the other end of the call, and proceed slowly. Articulate all the details and end the call. Most likely, the parent on the other end is disappointed and uncertain what to say. She will most likely address the situation with her child.

3. **Unconcerned.** Some parents will listen to what you are telling them and agree without concern, saying things like, "I'm not surprised," or "that's just the way he is." In these circumstances, there is little you can do other than relay the news and document the conversation. If the parent is not concerned and does not find the behavior or performance to be an issue, you probably will not be able to change his mind.

4. **Over-reacting.** On the other end of the spectrum, there will be parents who immediately want to identify and fix the problem, jumping to the worst possible conclusions as to why something happened. Your best bet is to help this parent say calm, by clearly stating the issue and explaining how you want to approach the issue from your standpoint.

Realize that although a phone call may be the most effective and necessary form of communication, it will not always be easy. Stay calm and do not let the person on the other end of the phone get the better of your emotions. That sounds easier than it is. Nonetheless, remember the following when delivering bad news over the phone:

- Wait to call when you are able to stay calm.
- Deliver the news simply and stick to the facts.

- Offer your suggestion for how you want to approach the issue.
- Thank the other person for his or her time and get off the phone as soon as you can.
- Document everything.

Face-to-face meetings

Phone calls for bad news can seem difficult, but you always have the option of getting off of the phone. Sometimes an issue warrants an actual meeting. The thought of discussing bad news with a parent in person is even more dismaying than delivering it over the phone.

For serious issues, face-to-face meetings are the most effective. The first challenge may be scheduling the meeting. You probably need to make a phone call to get it set up, and getting parents to agree to a time may depend on their work schedules. Additionally, you will have to use some other form of communication initially to set up the meeting. If you talk to them on the phone, you will need to provide some information up front. Be prepared to answer questions at that time. Additionally, remember to use positive word choices whenever possible so you do not put them on the defensive. Most of the time, you will be able to handle the meeting without concerns. Other times, you may have to deal with difficult people.

Tips for Dealing with Difficult Parents

Occasionally, even the best intentions will meet with resistance. In those circumstances, regardless of speaking on the phone or meeting in person, it is important to remain calm. The following are some effective strategies for neutralizing difficult situations with volatile individuals:

- In situations involving confrontation, always stay at eye level with the other person. If you sit and she stands, she will be looking down at you, allowing her the power in the situation. Ideally, both parties should be seated. In conflict scenarios, a new teacher should plan to have backup. In delicate face-to-face situations, it is recommended that you have a third party present, such as a principal.

- Try to keep your body language neutral, yet authoritative. Do not cross your arms or legs; doing so conveys that you are defensive or closed off. Do not fidget or touch your face during the conversation — these are signs of nervousness. In tense situations, subtly mirroring the body language of the other individual is one way to connect with them.

- Remain calm. A calm tone with neutral words is sometimes the best way to diffuse the situation. If you get angry at someone who is angry, this may only escalate the problem.

- Listen attentively, without interrupting. Wait until she is done talking. Sometimes, people just need to vent.

- When she is finished, calmly state the facts pertaining to the situation. Do not relay judgment or feelings.

- Respect the people you are talking with and expect them to respect what you are saying. Do not allow yourself to be bullied.

- If the other individual does attempt to bully you, stop the conversation. Calmly state that you do not permit anyone to speak with you in that tone of voice. Allow the person a minute or two to calm down and collect herself. If she does, continue with the meeting. If she cannot stop yelling, end the meeting. Do this by calmly and quietly walking away.

- It is of utmost importance that you always conduct yourself calmly and professionally. Even if you feel like a bundle of emotion on the inside, never let them see you sweat.

Dealing with parents is probably one of the hardest parts of the job. In particular, having to impart negative information about a student to his or her parent or guardian is not pleasant. On the other hand, it is very rewarding to be able to pass on praise and other positive statements about students. So, find ways to praise whenever possible. Doing so makes everyone feel better and it will give more credence to the less than positive remarks, if you are not always complaining about student performance and behavior.

"In my experience, verbal messages from a teacher are pretty easily forgotten. Teenagers are consumed with their own lives. Likewise, paper notifications are also easily lost or forgotten. In my opinion, an e-mail is sufficient in cases of an update or general information. If an issue is pressing, a phone call is the best means of communication.

In high school, I think it is important to hear from teachers when a student is falling below their capabilities. It is such a touchy time, even the smallest fluctuation in grades, participation, or attention could mean nothing, or it could be something major. I think teachers are better off to err on the side of caution. I remember one instance in particular. My husband is in the military, and while we were living in California at the time. I was at the school to pick up my daughter when a teacher waved me down in the parking lot to talk to me. He wanted to tell me that he had heard that my husband was in Iraq and knew how stressful things must be at home. He just wanted to be sure that I knew that my daughter was doing fine at school and that she was OK. That small effort meant the world to me, and I never forgot it.

— Paula Hernandez, parent

Chapter 9

Communicating with Administrators, Faculty, and Other Staff

"Argument is the worst sort of conversation."

— Jonathon Swift, Irish satirist, author of Gulliver's Travels (1667-1745)

As a teacher, you planned for a profession of teaching. You are probably very excited about stimulating minds and interacting with a wide array of students and personality types. That is fine, but what you may not have stopped to consider is the other half of the job. A large portion of the job involves interacting with administrators, other teachers, and a multitude of support staff. These interactions are critical to your success as a teacher. Build positive relationships with all of these individuals and you will have a very successful career. The first step to building these relationships is to understand who these people are and the types of interactions you will have with them. One of the smartest things you can do as a new teacher is to find allies among the staff. Make a positive first impression and develop good working relationships with everyone on the staff.

Hierarchy and Roles of Administration

Every school has its own distinct hierarchy. It depends on the type of school, the location, the size, and financial status of the district. Most public schools are run by a group of elected individuals known as a school board. To determine more about your school's individual hierarchy, contact the school board or review the information that is available online.

CASE STUDY: WHAT YOU NEED TO KNOW ABOUT SCHOOL DISTRICT HIERARCHIES

Richard Bradley
School Board Member
Mechanicsburg Area School District
www.mbgsd.org

Richard Bradley is one of the nine members on the Mechanicsburg Area School Board. He is currently serving his first term on the board. Bradley's case study provides insight into a typical school district hierarchy and the resulting pay scales. He provides information pertaining to the factors that go into agreeing on a teacher's salary from the school board's perspective.

As in most industries, the higher the degree one holds, the higher the pay scale. Most people in the school district administrative positions, such as the superintendent, financial officer, and principal, have at least a master's degree, and in most cases they also have a doctorate. It is not a job requirement for administrators to go beyond a master's degree, but in most cases, it is a requirement for applying for certain higher positions.

Teachers' salaries are based on a standard range for the school district and its surrounding area. Many factors go into setting the range. Information is gathered and judged against a broad spectrum of criteria implemented by the state. In Pennsylvania, teachers are covered under a union contract that establishes ranges for years of experience, degrees, and area of expertise. Salary increases are negotiated through a four-year contract. There are local divisions of national and state teacher unions representing each given school district. Since there are 501 school districts in Pennsylvania, there is a wide range of teacher salaries.

For school district administrators and support personnel, pay scales are based on a range consisting of a minimum and a maximum for each category of job being performed. Administrators are salaried employees, while most of the administrative support staffers, such as teachers' assistants, secretaries, building aides, food service workers, and custodians, are paid on an hourly wage basis. Hourly employees are also each placed in specific wage earning ranges, and paid accordingly.

The following is generally the order of pay. This example is relevant to our school district. Other districts may have additional positions not included in this list. As stated above, this is an example, but the pay can vary because of the ranges and is dependent on years of service, experience level, and degrees held by the individual.

Salaried school district hierarchy:

- *Superintendent:* The chief school administrator oversees the district and has executive power and administration rights within the school district.
- *Chief Fiscal Officer:* The chief fiscal officer is essentially a treasurer of sorts for the school district. They handle the money that comes in from the federal and state tax bureaus. They must understand all of the current state and federal regulations.
- *Assistant Superintendent:* The second in command to the superintendent has responsibilities in grant writing, staff development, curriculum design, assessment supervision, budget development, and technology.
- *Directors of Student Services:* A member of the superintendent's senior management team. Oversees the district's guidance program, nursing services, IEP and 504 coordination, home schooling, and student appeal processes, as well as supervise the school principals.
- *High School and Middle School Principals:* Responsible for administering policies and procedures, develop school budgets, implement school site programs, confer with staff on curriculums, evaluate classroom instructors, and handle safety concerns.
- *Elementary School Principals:* Oversee the day-to-day running of their schools. Hire and evaluate teachers, prepare budgets, develop academic programs.

- *Assistant Principals at all levels:* Assist principals, administer school student personnel programs, counsel and discipline students, supervise student activity programs, supervise guidance, maintain student attendance, and oversee student and substitute teachers.
- *Technology Director:* Oversees district's technology department, including purchasing, maintenance and repair of computer networks, video/audio equipment, and other systems.
- *School Psychologists:* Responsible for testing students who may qualify for special needs services, make recommendation on adaptations for students in the classroom, and work with guidance counselors and teachers to assist students.
- *Directors of Athletics, Facility, and Food Services:* These individuals are responsible for overseeing their respective departments and the individuals who work in them.
- *Teachers:* To reiterate, the teacher scale is broad and wide. The pay can range from the lowest level of the hierarchy all the way up to the assistant principal's level. It depends on education, years of experience, and the district. Each district has a different pay scale.

Hourly school district hierarchy:

- Administrative assistants to the central district office
- Administrative assistants to the school
- Administrative aides
- Special education instructional aides
- Food service employees
- Custodial employees
- Teacher's aides

In addition to the positions listed above, most districts have a group of individuals set up as a governing board, known as the school board. This is a group of elected officials. In respect to the overall job title hierarchy and chain of command, the school board has final say on all decisions affecting the school district, including hiring and firing. For the most part, this is simply a formality, but it provides a means of checks and balances. It is usually an unpaid position.

Decision-making school district hierarchy:

School Board
Superintendent
Chief Fiscal
Assistant Superintendent
Directors of Student Services
High School Principals
Middle School Principals
Elementary School Principals
Assistant Principals at all levels
Directors
School Psychologists and guidance staff
Teachers
Administrative staff
Other support staff

The U.S. Department of Education ensures that all government-funded schools function under a local legislative authority. They are known as school districts, under whose auspices you as a public school teacher will find work. A district covers a geographic area, sometimes by county, sometimes by town, and in places such as Louisiana, by parish. A school board, with a superintendent and elected officials, heads the district. The district serves as the deciding factor on everything from funding distribution — including teacher salaries — to higher-level student disciplinary actions such as expulsion. Each district reports back to its respective state, and each state reports back to the United States Department of Education, which tallies and reports statistics. This information includes how many schools or students should be in a particular district, the racial and economic makeup of any given district, and the amount of funding spent on special programs. Visit **www.ed.gov** to find information on the specific district you are interested in.

The school board

A school board or board of education is a select group of individuals elected for decision-making purposes in a particular school system. They determine and enforce policy and oversee the administration by providing a system of checks and balances. The board dictates policy for a specific region of schools, such as a district, city, or other pre-determined area.

The school board will have a mission statement for the schools it directs. It will define what your district expects from its teachers. The statement serves as a relevant guide on which to base goals for you, your school, and your students. As a new teacher, you should attend school board meetings in order to become familiar with how the district facilitates and maintains the integrity of its mission statement. You also will get to know the individuals who comprise the school board, and you will understand how policies are implemented.

Districts post meeting schedules on their Web sites or in their newsletters, and these meetings often are held on the same day of each week or month, during evening hours. They are public forums, and anyone is invited to attend. This is a great way to find out how your district works. Citizens, teachers, and students may share their opinions with prior notification, so meetings tend to be long and drawn-out when controversial issues are on the floor. You might find everything from subsidy debates to calendar decisions, and perhaps even people protesting the latest teaching trend or funding fiasco. This edification is well worth your time.

Department chairs

Since high school encompasses multiple grades and many subjects within each grade, most high schools have individuals who oversee each department, such as math, science, foreign language, and so forth. It is usually a veteran teacher well-versed in the school's policies and procedures, as well as the subject matter. This person is the department chair. High school department chairpersons are in charge of various duties, primarily the care and tracking of textbooks and bringing information from the principal or district back to the teachers in the department during regularly scheduled department meetings. In some schools, they may also be in charge of the supplies for the teachers in the subject area.

Keep in mind: These individuals have teaching duties along with their departmental duties. They are incredibly busy during the first days of school, with accommodating other teachers and preparing their classrooms. In most schools, they also receive an extra stipend for this position, so ask if you need something. Early in your classroom-preparation days, check that you have enough textbooks and a teacher edition for each one. This way, you can give yourself plenty of time to let your department head know you understand that he or she is busy and that you would like to go to the bookroom or supply room to get what you need at his or her convenience.

Teachers

Finding a mentor

Some school districts have mentors for their beginning teachers; others do not. If you are beginning a new job without a mentor, look for a teacher who has high standards. You will know this teacher by his or her sincerity in loving his or her job and the consistency of a good attitude. This teacher will have no problem being observed by other teachers. A good mentor will be excited to share ideas and knowledge with you, and this person will be someone of good humor and enthusiastic about teaching.

Hopefully, you have taken the time to meet as many of your colleagues as possible in the few weeks you are preparing your room before the first day of school. The best way to find a mentor is to pay attention toe the other teachers every day. Listen to what they have to say during lunch and if you have free time once school begins, try to observe how they interact with their students. An effective mentor will be happy to take you under his or her wing and fill you in on every tip and resource imaginable. He or she will be more than willing to listen to your concerns about curriculum issues, where to find materials for activities, what administration and parents expect of you, how to work with the parents in your community, and how to create good lesson plans. There will never be too many questions for an effective mentor to answer, and he or she will never make you feel uncomfortable asking for help.

While it is true some veteran teachers do not like beginning teachers, there are just as many who are enthusiastic about helping a new staff member. Try not to be intimidated by unenthusiastic veteran teachers. Some veteran teachers, have a "wait and see" approach to interacting with new teachers. Because a large percentage of rookie teachers end up leaving the profession, some veteran teachers choose not to invest their time and energy on a new teacher until they believe he has what it takes to stick with the job.

The importance of a mentor cannot be overstated. You will be overwhelmed with the daily demands, piles of paperwork, periodic meetings, and insurmountable memos. These are the things you will need to talk about with someone who has experienced it.

Heed strong advice from veteran teachers when they say you should be careful of labeling students before you know them. It is possible the student had a bad year or two and has finally passed the hurdle of bad behavior. On the other hand, it is good to know if you possibly have a kleptomaniac in your classroom.

Students who have connections should be handled carefully. One of your students may be the child of your principal or the superintendent, so tread lightly. You should treat all your students equally, but it is advisable to be especially cautious in following protocol with these students.

Teacher mentoring programs

Inexperienced teachers sometimes ask exactly who becomes a mentor and why. That is a question Florida's Brevard County public school leaders have answered. Brevard County's school system has a principal leadership program and a teacher induction program — both proving to be successful. In Brevard County schools, all new teachers go through the induction program and are mentored by a veteran teacher. The reason is easily understood when you read the school system's mission statement: "Our mission is to serve every student with excellence as the standard."

So who are these people that become mentors? According to Brevard County schools, they are "high-performing, experienced teachers." These teachers are veterans who work closely with new teachers, guiding them while giving continuous coaching and constructive feedback. In Brevard County schools, mentors are expected to:

- Foster a supportive and positive relationship with mentored colleague(s)
- Participate in meetings and activities with the new teacher that introduces them to the school and faculty
- Share knowledge, expertise, and constructive guidance
- Conduct two formative observations
- Act as primary resource for the new teacher and offer specific information

One of the most important reasons for schools to have a teacher-mentoring program was because studies have shown that mentoring teachers is interrelated with the retention of new teachers in the profession. The studies seem to indicate teacher-mentoring programs are a key factor in convincing teachers to stay in the profession, and it is believed that the reason the program works is because new teachers do not feel so overwhelmed when there is a mentor to help them understand and organize in order to meet the job's demands. Making the workload more manageable is how mentors help the most because the workload is the leading cause of stress in a new teacher's life.

The mentoring program for teachers also improves student achievement because of the help new teachers get in lesson planning, organization, and preparation. One of the biggest problems mentors face is the same problem all teachers face: lack of time. If possible, plan to meet with your mentor on a regular basis. There will be times this will not be possible, and as a fellow teacher who struggles to have enough time of your own, this should be perfectly understandable. Help your mentor by using e-mail or calling only in the evening. You might find that your mentor is a morning person and you could meet for coffee and doughnuts before school once a week. This would give you time to relax and enjoy the camaraderie you will share through your love of teaching. There is also the possibility of car-pooling, giving you time to talk on the way to school and again on the way home. This also leaves the time that you have set aside for the morning and afternoon free to accomplish tasks.

The teacher induction program has helped Broward County teachers blend into the new job with ease. Dr. Haim Ginott, a teacher, child psychologist, and psychotherapist who worked with children and parents, reviewed the program and also pioneered techniques for conversing with children still taught today. His words of wisdom: "I have come to the frightening conclusion that I am the decisive element in the classroom. It is my personal approach that creates the climate. It is my daily mood that makes the weather. As a teacher I possess tremendous power to make a child's life miserable or joyous. I can be a tool of torture or an instrument of inspiration. I can humiliate or humor, hurt or heal. In all situations it is my response that decides whether a crisis will be escalated or de-escalated, and a child is humanized or de-humanized."

When reading over Ginott's quote, one realizes the power a teacher has is as strong as that of a parent. If the position of a teacher is so powerful in the lives of our children, why would we not want to make that first year teacher as qualified and effective as possible? According to the National Education Association, "Evidence strongly suggests that mentoring improves the quality of teaching." Many schools are now in the second generation of the mentoring program. The first generation was a learning experience for all involved, and much was learned from the first ones who jumped in with an effort to help new teachers.

Unfortunately, those first mentors were not trained and it was sometimes an overwhelming experience for the veteran teachers as well as the induction teachers. Now, with the second generation of mentors helping new teachers, it has been found that sometimes mentors need mentors. Today, teachers who have been mentors train the teachers who sign up to be mentors.

Phyllis Williams was a first generation mentor and is now a member of the professional development committee for United Teachers Los Angeles. When thinking back on those days of being a new mentor, Williams said, "In my first year of mentoring, I felt like a new teacher. The information was given to us quickly and I felt lost. You are fumbling around trying to look like a mentor, but what you really need is someone to mentor the mentor."

Teachers who wish to become mentors complete a training program so they are better prepared to help new teachers. The payoff for mentoring accumulates over time. The longer we have mentors, the more we learn about what is needed by new teachers and students, and the better the mentors become. When the mentorship programs improve, so does the quality of the new teachers. With effective teachers comes better achievement of the students.

The problems you will face in your first year of teaching will not all be solved, but having a mentor will help eliminate many of those problems and ease the discomfort brought on by those problems not solved right away. When you are feeling doubtful of remaining in the profession, a good mentor will point out your strengths, help you build a good dialogue with your students, and ease the headaches of whether your lesson plans need improvement. With continuous feedback on how to improve and what you are doing right, you are certain to have a successful first year as an elementary teacher.

The buddy system

If you hear of another new teacher in the building, you may want to find him or her and introduce yourself. No one understands what you are experiencing better than someone who is going through the same thing. It will give comfort to both of you when you need it most, encouragement when you feel like quitting, humor when outsiders do not understand, and feedback when it cannot be found anywhere else. There will be times when your profession will make you feel isolated and lonely, and having another beginning teacher to discuss these feelings with will greatly ease that discomfort.

Support staff

Without support staff, our schools would crumble. Take a look around your classroom. Someone made sure these tasks were accomplished:

- The room is clean.
- Your students have enough desks.
- Someone moved the desks into the classroom for you.
- You have keys to your classroom.

- Your W2-form information is entered into the district payroll department's ledger.
- The front desk holds parents at bay so you can prepare your classroom before being stampeded with questions and concerns for their children's new teacher.
- You received the correct class rosters with your students on it.
- You received a copy of the faculty handbook.
- You are entered in the district's list of global e-mail addresses.

Teaching is not a solo gig. However, because the job is often quite challenging, we overlook the encumbrance of others and do not give the kind of recognition our support staff so often deserve. The individuals we work with outside of the classroom are often the power behind our success inside the classroom, and a simple hello, smile, or even a box of doughnuts goes a long way. At the very least, make your requests polite.

Guidance counselors/school psychologists

High school guidance counselors have multiple responsibilities. One of their primary responsibilities is to prepare the students for what comes next. They provide information about job placement programs, vocational/technological programs, and college programs. They deal with testing and setting up visits with the people who work in these industries. They are involved with compiling student grades, class ranks, and activities. They also have experience with dealing with other issues that may impact their education. They are involved with preparing education plans for students with any special requirements, such as IEPs and 504 plans. They also work closely with the school psychologist and the school nurses on other issues that may involve seeking outside assistance such as abuse, thoughts of suicide, and substance dependency.

The federal government recommends one counselor per every 250 students in the school. There is a huge discrepancy in this area. According to a 2009 study of the American Counseling Association, the actual average in the United States is currently 475:1, with many schools having even worse ratios. The chart below depicts the ratio of counselors to students per state in the United States.

United States Student-to-Counselor Ratios	
Alabama	398:1
Alaska	452:1
Arizona	750:1
Arkansas	339:1
California	809:1
Colorado	470:1
Connecticut	409:1
Delaware	451:1
District of Columbia	356:1
Florida	433:1
Georgia	448:1
Hawaii	273:1
Idaho	443:1
Illinois	1,076:1
Indiana	543:1
Iowa	400:1
Kansas	418:1
Kentucky	454:1
Louisiana	225:1
Maine	315:1
Maryland	349:1
Massachusetts	426:1
Michigan	643:1
Minnesota	777:1
Mississippi	464:1
Missouri	337:1
Montana	310:1
Nebraska	369:1
Nevada	484:1
New Hampshire	243:1
New Jersey	495:1
New Mexico	404:1
New York	463:1
North Dakota	366:1

Ohio	493:1
Oklahoma	391:1
Oregon	485:1
Pennsylvania	380:1
Rhode Island	360:1
South Carolina	407:1
South Dakota	390:1
Tennessee	357:1
Texas	430:1
Utah	772:1
Vermont	220:1
Virginia	300:1
Washington	500:1
West Virginia	405:1
Wisconsin	454:1
Wyoming	203:1

What was once known as the library is now the "media center." It is not only filled with books, but also computers and other digital equipment. The media specialist is the gatekeeper to all of these valuable educational tools. Some teachers seem to forget it is still a library. The media center is for research, checking out books, and computer testing if terminals are not available in the teacher's classroom. It is not a student dumping ground. Teachers need to find out from the media specialist how many students are acceptable to send at one time.

Front-office staff

On some days, the front counter is more aptly described as the front lines. The receptionists are answering the phones, while teachers are buzzing for attention on the intercom. Substitutes are waiting to see where they need to go next, while parents are impatiently glaring. In many middle schools, there is no school nurse, and the front-office clerks also have the responsibility of acting as emergency medical technicians.

Custodians

Custodians are charged with everything from mowing the lawn to keeping the bathroom sanitary. They empty the garbage after school, clean the toilets, scrub graffiti off walls, and scrape gum off the bottoms of desks. Obviously, their tasks are not always pleasant. Custodians appreciate the people who make their lives a little easier. After each class, take a minute before the bell to make sure all materials are put away and books are off the floor.

The school nurse

School nursing is unique as it combines nursing with academic concerns. According to the National Association of School Nurses (NASN), school nurses "...facilitate normal development; promote health and safety; intervene with actual and potential health problems; provide case management services; and actively collaborate with others to build student and family capacity for adaptation, self management, self advocacy, and learning."

School nursing has changed dramatically over the last decade. More students with chronic conditions and disabilities are attending mainstream schools. Therefore, the understanding of conditions, warning signs, and medicine disbursement falls on the school nurses shoulders. This is in addition to the traditional stomach bug and twisted ankles.

Despite changes in the nursing field overall, school nurses are still predominantly women. The job includes aspects of being a parent, a doctor, a counselor, and even a physical therapist. School nurses still perform vision and hearing tests and conduct height and weight assessments. In 2009, school nurses across the country were given the daunting task of screening and inoculating students and faculty against the swine flu. Additionally, the average school nurse has daily responsibilities in assisting students with diabetes, asthma, arthritis, attention-deficit hyperactivity disorder (ADHD), severe allergies, autism, and a host of physical disabilities. At any given time, she may need to assist someone with a catheter, respirator, insulin pump, or even feeding tube.

Given the additional responsibilities, the federal government recommends that each school have one nurse for every group of 750 typical healthy students. The sanction cites healthy students because certain diagnoses require schools to have additional nursing staff on hand. Unfortunately, there is a national nursing shortage. Therefore, despite the government proposal, the average school nurse in the United States is responsible for more than 1,100 students in two different buildings. At some schools in this country, secretaries and building aides are asked to cover for nurses when they are out of the building.

CASE STUDY: WHAT DO NEW TEACHERS NEED TO KNOW FROM THE NURSE'S PERSPECTIVE?

Linda Weaver
High School Nurse Substitute
Central PA school districts

Linda Weaver is hospital nurse with 20 years experience and an expertise in cardiac issues. She is also a mother of three children, two of whom are teenagers. When she became a parent, she changed her full-time nursing status to part-time so that she could spend more time with her children. Over the years, she has acted as the nurse on site in multiple camps, on various school field trips, and as a substitute nurse in many schools at all levels.

I love working in the schools because I really like being with the kids. Of all the levels, working in the high school is the most challenging. The full-time nurse at the high school I work in is amazing. In addition to being a nurse, I have seen her act in the capacity of parent, confidant, and social worker.

A typical day at the high school starts with students coming in for their routine medications, such as ADD medicine. Soon after that, they start arriving with fevers, headaches, and stomach problems. Much of the day is spent giving out over-the-counter pain relievers and throat lozenges, just like in the elementary and middle schools. In the high school, however, there are a lot more severe issues to deal with. In addition to broken bones and dislocated shoulders from physical education and sport practices, there are girls who are pregnant and students who suffer from various forms of abuse.

Many of the kids who have to be sent home drive themselves home and go to empty houses, where they essentially have to take care of themselves. In one instance, I encountered a student who lived alone in his own apartment.

The school has a computer that provides information on each student in case there is a major diagnosis like asthma or diabetes. Additionally, there are notes in the office about certain students who frequent the nurse's office for other reasons.

There is information pertaining to kids who are "cutters," anorexic, or pregnant. This information is not on the computer file, but is kept in a secure location so the substitute nurses and aides know what is going on if they come in.

Sometimes, the nurse's office is simply a refuge for students who feel overwhelmed. They want to talk about problems at home or just need a place to lie down for a little while. The nurse sometimes acts as a liaison between the student and the guardian. They will help talk to parents in discussing news about pregnancy, or another recently discussed condition. They may help set up doctor's appointments as well.

In addition to standard emergency equipment, there are items to help disabled children take care of their issues, such as lifts in the bathroom. Most kids at this age are very independent and do not want help unless they absolutely need it. You have to remember that most of them are adult-sized at this point.

The hardest thing I have ever encountered as a substitute nurse is a school code blue. There was a student who had a seizure in class. He literally fell on the teacher who did not understand what was going on. They called a code blue and a team of teachers and health care professionals responded very quickly to the emergency. Each year, there are a team of teachers and staff who are trained to respond to student emergencies. Some of the personnel are EMTs trained in CPR and AED use. When a code blue is called, all members of the team react quickly and professionally to come to a student's aid. In the hospital setting, it is Intensive Care Unit (ICU) nurse and doctors who handle code blue situations. High schools today train and prepare team members to handle emergency situations allowing for positive student outcomes.

My advice for a new teacher would be: Get to know your students and never be afraid to ask for help. In the beginning, it is hard to know whom to trust and when to believe a student. The bottom line is, it is always safer to err on the side of caution. Send the student to the nurse.

If the individual should be in class, the nurse will send him or her right back to class. Also, get acquainted with your school's code blue team and the correct procedures for specific emergencies in your school.

If you notice patterns that concern you, such as frequent trips to the bathroom, repeated episodes of falling asleep in class, a sudden change in behavior, or signs of isolation and depression, never hesitate to let the nurse know. You will probably be informed about certain student medical conditions if it involves something you may see in your classroom, such as an insulin pump. Usually this occurs when students have IEPs or 504 plans. There may be many other circumstances that you are not aware of. Again, never hesitate to contact the nurse or one of the counselors if you are concerned.

There are several reasons to send student to the school nurse, but what you may not realize is there is a high percentage chance that they will return to your classroom before the period is over. School nurses are trained in dealing with all kinds of illnesses and other issues. Therefore, unless a student has a high fever, an obvious injury, or has been seen throwing up, he most likely will not be sent home.

Section 4:

Matters You Cannot Control

"It is, in fact, nothing short of a miracle that the modern methods of instruction have not entirely strangled the holy curiosity of inquiry."

— Albert Einstein, theoretical physicist (1879-1955)

By this time, you know what the job entails, whom you are working with, and how to teach your class. It seems pretty simple and straightforward. But you are not quite there yet. Now it is time for you to discover myriad truths that no one told you about in school — the factors you have no control over.

Chapter 10

Politics in Education

What You Need to Understand

Although you report to the schools' administration and have to answer to the school board, there are actually other factions in charge of your job. Educating the youth of America is a very involved process. It is also a costly affair. You have heard that taxpayers pay teachers' salaries, but how exactly does that work?

Control and funding for education in America comes from three places: federal, state, and local governments. Despite being responsible for the allocation of funds, the government is not involved in setting curriculum. This is a very good thing, especially when you consider there are more than 5,000 employees in the U.S. Department of Education. Having to deal with 5,000 ideas for creating curriculum would be an overwhelming task. Nevertheless, the government does impact the amount of funding each school receives. They determine how much money each district is allowed to have from federal funding. The state also has a say in how much funding certain schools will receive from the state funds.

Understanding mandates

A mandate is essentially a law. It is an obligation handed down by some form of government. In terms of education, there are a lot of mandates that affect those teaching in public schools. Although some issues affect all forms of education, most relate only to public schools. This is the one of the primary differences between public schools, charter schools, and private institutions. The government essentially provides funding for public schools, and as such they indicate what outcomes they expect.

The mandates appear at three different levels: Federal legislation, state legislation, and local regulations. In this section, the mandated areas are broken down into these three areas and explained in detail. All of these are pertinent to public school teachers. Any lesson plans must take these regulations into consideration.

No Child Left Behind (NCLB)

As a teacher, you understand that the state and the district mandate the standards you cover in your classroom. These standards are set so your students can better meet the level the federal government set in the No Child Left Behind act (NCLB). In 2002, under President George H. W. Bush's administration, NCLB was passed into law with intentions of getting all students' performances up to their grade level or beyond by the year 2014. The act requires assessments in different subjects at certain grade levels. These assessments are to be acquired during specified years set by the government. One example of such an assessment is the Ohio Graduation Test (OGT). Before students can graduate from high school and receive a diploma, they must pass this test.

NCLB legislation is set up to start working with students from the early grades. A large part of NCLB regulations are concerned with grades 3 through 8, with concentrated testing every year. Despite that, NCLB also pertains to high schools. The mandated regulations for high schools are as follows:

- **Each state must have annual achievement objectives.** The objectives must be met in such as way that there is a measurable improvement in performance. The goals must include proficiency in math and reading for all students by the end of the 2013 to 2014 school year. There are consequences for schools that do not comply. Each school is expected to meet their objectives for two years in a row. If they do not succeed, they have two years to correct the issue. At that time, parents may pull their students out and send them to other schools. If the objectives remain unmet for five years, the government may restructure the school and staff or close the school.

- **Objectives need to consider socio-economic indicators.** States must create separate standards for certain students. They are students with disabilities, minorities, low-income students, and students with limited-language abilities.

- **High school objectives include graduation rate accountability.** The mandate requires adequate yearly progress shown in graduation rates. The NCLB laws stipulate that alternative diplomas and GED certifications do not count in the overall graduation rate.

- **The test objective must be made between tenth and twelfth grade.** The annual testing objective is different in high school. The law states that testing must occur in at least one grade between tenth and twelfth grades. Students are tested in math, reading, and science. Exceptions and modifications are made for disabled students and those with limited language capabilities. Most high schools give this test during junior year (eleventh grade).

- **Schools should expect teachers who teach core subjects to meet the states' "highly qualified" status.** Core subjects are defined as including English, reading, language arts; math, science; foreign languages; government and civics; economics; arts; history; and geography. The status requirements are: hold at least one bachelor's degree, full certification, demonstrated subject competence, and be in continuing education.

It is important to note that NCLB does not require high school seniors to pass an exit exam or to earn a diploma. Instead, the legislation places emphasis on meeting the goals of improvement in testing and the amount of people graduating.

Essentially, this puts a larger burden on teachers to cover all the necessary information. You have probably heard the expression, "teaching to the test." That means, as a new teacher, you have to make sure you cover everything your students will need for the standards testing. It may seem overwhelming when you are creating your lesson plans. Keep in mind that other teachers have been doing it for several years now, so it is possible

In order to assist your students, you must first accept the importance of these standards. If you do not believe in the standards you are teaching, your teaching skills will be affected, you will not be the most effective teacher you can be, and your students may not do well on the mandated tests.

Each state must create standards outlining the material your students will master by the end of the school year in order to pass to the next grade level. You, as a teacher, must design a course of study for your students to meet those standards. This is the foundation of your lesson plans. Having your students master those standards should be your objective because this will be the gauge that determines whether your students are successful.

You may have to listen to some student and parent complaints. Some students do not test well and others will fly through the tests with no problem. It is something that has been going on for many years now, however, so most people accept it for what it is.

The Individuals with Disabilities Education Act (IDEA)

Mandating standards ensures that baseline criteria are met for students. What about the students who are way above and way below the baseline — what happens to them? Parents, teachers, and administrators all over the country asked these questions. Eventually, new regulations were passed to provide rights for all students with other needs. Bureaucratic rights have since been established protecting the rights of parents of special needs children so they have a voice in their children's education. Rights have also been established to protect the students and ensure their educational rights. What has come from these laws and rights is better known as "inclusion."

In 1975, Congress enacted the Individuals with Disabilities Education Act (IDEA). The purpose of the legal action was to guarantee the opportunity of appropriate free public education for children with disabilities. Many updates were made to the law before its final regulations were published in 2006.

One of the most important amendments came into fruition in 1997. IDEA was amended and schools were required to educate special needs children in regular classrooms whenever possible. The Individual Education Plan (IEP) requirement for all special needs children was implemented. A team of teachers, administrators, parents, counselors, and outside experts must develop the IEP. The student for which the plan is developed is also part of the IEP team. Together, this team creates a learning plan that stresses the special needs of the child so their educational needs are met.

It may seem to some people that the number of students with special needs is minimal, but approximately half the current population of the United States is affected by disabilities, either themselves or through association.

People who create learning programs for teaching degrees are now encouraged to change said programs in order to include inclusion concepts. For example, the inclusion concept could be educating a teacher to know how to deal with an autistic child. Without proper training, the teachers could be at a loss. Teachers who have been successful with inclusion classrooms have stated that resources, time, and training were the determining factors in their accomplishments. With inclusion being the standard in all classrooms, the concepts of teaching and learning must adapt for the benefit of both teachers and students.

Special Education Local Plan Areas (SELPA)

States provide a minimum basic special education allocation. This funding is based on a per pupil amount for a district's entire student population. Funds for special education services are distributed through Special Education Local Plan Areas (SELPA). Under certain circumstances, charter schools also receive funds through SELPA.

With budget cuts and slashed funding, it may be more difficult for teachers to find resources to teach special needs students. Regardless of the burden prompted by budget cuts, it is a law by which teachers must abide. In 2005-2006, regular education spending totaled less than $10,000 per pupil in elementary and secondary schools. According to The Center for Special Education Finance, the total spending used to educate the average student with a disability amounts to approximately $12,500 per pupil, depending on the state.

Another special needs area is "English as a Second Language" students, for which the U.S. Supreme Court established English Language Learners (ELL) rights by passing the Education Opportunity Act of 1974. School districts are now required to address linguistic deficiencies of language minorities.

Through all of these state and federal requirements you must meet, please keep in mind your administrators are there to help you succeed. Your success is their success, and all of you are working together to achieve the same goal.

Council for Exceptional Children (CEC)

In 2007, Congressman Gallegly of California introduced the Gifted and Talented Students Education Act. The legislation allows the allocation of resources to pay for gifted education. The legal action came as a result of NCLB. Opponents believed that advanced learners were being neglected because of NCLB.

Budget cuts in education

Despite an effort by the last couple government administrations to improve student and school performance, there have been numerous budget cuts in school programs. It appears that education spending is one of the first things cut when there is an economic downturn. The juxtaposition can sometimes create challenges for administrators and educators. For example:

- In 2006, President Bush made a proposal to cut education spending by more than $3 billion dollars, but at the same time he wanted to strengthen math and science programs.

- California once had an educational system touted as a national model. Governor Arnold Schwarzenegger; however, is planning to cut the education budget by $1.3 billion in the 2009 school year and $4 billion the following year; California schools will drastically change.

- In Florida, a state that already struggles due to lack of funding, administrators were reported to say the budget cuts were "bleeding the education system." Students and teachers all over central Florida rallied together and wore red shirts to represent their discontentment with the massive education budget cut of $100 million in February 2009. Governor Charlie Crist stated he was waiting for a waiver from the Secretary of Education to get the federal stimulus money for education. Last reported, Florida was not eligible to receive the stimulus money because the state does not fund education enough to qualify; however, a waiver was granted on May 11, 2009, allowing the sunshine state access to funding.

American Act and Reinvestment Act of 2009

President Obama's administration is working to find ways to ease the burden for teachers and at the same time improve the quality of education the students receive. Obama is attempting to begin this process through his American Recovery and Reinvestment Act of 2009. The official Web site of the Department of Education (www.ed.gov) reads, "The Act is an extraordinary response to a crisis unlike any since the Great Depression, and includes measures to modernize our nation's infrastructure, enhance energy independence, expand educational opportunities, preserve and improve affordable health care, provide tax relief, and protect those in greatest need." The site goes on to state that President Obama is "committed to providing every child access to a complete and competitive education, from cradle through career."

With the American Recovery and Reinvestment Act, there will be:

- $5 billion for early learning programs, including programs for children with special needs
- $77 billion for reforms to strengthen elementary and secondary education, including $48.6 billion to stabilize state education budgets
- $5 billion in competitive funds to spur innovation

With the American Recovery and Reinvestment Act, $77 billion has been earmarked for reform to strengthen elementary and secondary education and is also to be used for encouraging states to "make improvements in teacher effectiveness and ensure that all schools have highly qualified teachers." President Obama indicated that education is a priority to his administration. He called teachers "the single most important resource to a child's learning." He vows to ensure "that teachers are supported as professionals in the classroom." This act offers new teachers promise and recognition.

The push for charter schools

One area that has received attention and praise from Obama's administration is the creation of new charter schools. Many charter schools have been very successful, particularly in urban areas. The President wants to see continued progress in the American education system, and his administration sees the creation of additional charter schools as a step in the right direction. Given the administration's push for more charter schools, the teacher unions have reacted, wanting more charter school teachers to unionize. Previously, most charter schools did not need to worry about government intervention or unions, so it remains to be seen what kind of impact they will have on the future of charter schools in the country.

Education is constantly changing

In 2006, the National Center on Education and the Economy assembled a panel of bipartisan education and policy experts. The result is a pilot project at dozens of high schools in eight different states. The project, starting in Fall 2010, will provide board exams for tenth grade students. After passing the boards, these students would have the option to get a diploma two years early so they could enroll in a community college. If the students wanted to attend more selective colleges, they could take college preparatory course during their junior and senior years.

The board exams will cover English, math, science, and history. Connecticut, Maine, New Hampshire, Vermont, Rhode Island, Kentucky, New Mexico, and Pennsylvania will test the project. The Bill and Melinda Gates foundation granted $1.5 million to the national center to help get the program started. The money will help cover the cost of the material and the teacher training.

Chapter 11

A Dose of Reality

There is no specific personality profile that fits every teacher. You may be a young, wide-eyed, optimistic college graduate excited to take on the challenges of the modern classroom. You may be a mid-career professional who is generally cynical about the world in general. You may think you know how teenagers think. You may truly believe that you are prepared for anything and that nothing could shock you. Regardless of what you learned in school, or even in life so far, you have no idea what you have gotten yourself into.

Unfortunately, there are numerous individuals out there who were once teachers but quit.

They leave the profession because they feel overworked, underpaid, overwhelmed, and underappreciated. Many cite their personal frustrations with the National Education Association and/or the U.S. Department of Education. There are complaints of poor working conditions. These conditions can encompass anything from building problems to crowded classrooms. Other concerns include out-of-date textbooks and materials, inadequate planning time, excess of unnecessary meetings, and of course, insufficient pay. It sounds dismal, but it is better to prepare for the worst.

So how do you survive? Talk to veteran teachers who are still passionate about their jobs. If possible, sit in on their classes. Negative attitudes are contagious, but thankfully, so is positive energy. It is fine to know the potential downside of the job, but also have a plan for visiting the upside as often as possible.

Luckily, the profession is filled with optimists. Surround yourself with as many as you can — and as often as possible. Veteran teachers who have a positive attitude can offer you a wealth of information, as well as inspiration to keep going.

Armed with Rhetoric

You start the job armed with plans and ideals. You have reviewed your notes from school and believe you are ready for your new career as a teacher. General Education programs may differ in specifications, but they all boast preparedness for teaching. The program descriptions usually include rhetoric similar to these objectives listed on one Pennsylvania university's Web site:

- Obtain a range of skills and knowledge
- Learn how to communicate effectively
- Understand the cultural movements shaping society
- Emerge from school as a knowledgeable, informed, literate individual
- Acquire knowledge through multiple critical-information gathering processes
- Participate in various opportunities to analyze and evaluate
- Encouraged to make critical judgments in a logical and rational manner
- Prepare for presentation, organization, and debate particular to appropriate discipline
- Comprehend concepts of international interdependence and cultural diversity

The curriculum sounds as if it will produce teachers prepared for anything. Unfortunately, even an Ivy League school such as Penn State cannot prepare you for everything. The pages that follow include some of the less-than-ideal scenarios you may encounter during your first year as a high school teacher.

On the plus side, you will only be new and inexperienced for a short period. In the mean time, remain flexible and positive and never lose your sense of humor.

The Cold Hard Facts

Teaching is hard work. Teaching high school students is especially hard. Unfortunately, many idealistic individuals leave the profession because their expectations do not coincide with reality. Here are facts you need to know:

- According to the National Center for Education Statistics (NCES), one out of every five first-year teachers leaves the profession within the first three years.
- Each year, 30 percent of new teachers entering the profession will leave after only two years.
- The proportion of new teachers who leave the profession in the first five years remains around 50 percent. This is a statistic that has existed for several decades, according to Barry A. Farber, a professor of education and psychology at Columbia University in New York.
- More than 50 percent will be gone by the end of seven years.
- The statistics for inner-city schools are even worse. Approximately 50 percent of new teachers in urban areas leave the profession within their first three years.

There are multiple reasons for the depressing statistics. There are two primary reasons most teachers cite to explain their departures from this noble profession. They receive insufficient earnings and poor working conditions. This is a very real problem in the United States. There is not enough money invested in educating the future generations. These are the people who will inherit the country and they are inadequately prepared. This is, however, not a new problem. This issue is one lamented by educators for the most of the last century. You may have heard these statistics before. These are the facts and you need to be aware of them as you enter the field of education. Times will be tough and the pay is not great. If you embrace this knowledge and keep a positive attitude, you will be able to survive and even succeed as a teacher.

Ask any working teacher about student teacher ratios, and they will tell you that the numbers are often misleading. These ratios do not directly correlate to actual class size. Schools use a formula for determining the ratio they quote in their literature. The formula divides the total student enrollment by the number of full-time-equivalent (FTE) teachers. FTE teachers range from those who teach a required course to those who teach electives, such as art and music.

Taking that in consideration, the following chart consists of the reported student/teacher ratio by state. Keep in mind that many variables affect this figure, and it may not be a good indication of how many students you will have in each of your classes. For more specific information, ask the secretary in the guidance office about class enrolment size.

STUDENT/TEACHER RATIO BY STATE	
Utah	22:1
Arizona	21:1
California	21:1
Oregon	21:1
Washington	19:1
Nevada	19:1
Michigan	18:1
Florida	18:1
Idaho	18:1
Alaska	17:1
Colorado	17:1
Indiana	17:1
Illinois	17:1
Hawaii	17:1
Minnesota	16:1
Kentucky	16:1
Oklahoma	16:1
Maryland	16:1

Georgia	16:1
Tennessee	16:1
South Carolina	15:1
Pennsylvania	15:1
Delaware	15:1
Ohio	15:1
Mississippi	15:1
Wisconsin	15:1
North Carolina	15:1
New Mexico	15:1
Texas	15:1
Arkansas	15:1
Kansas	14:1
Louisiana	14:1
Montana	14:1
West Virginia	14:1
Missouri	14:1
District of Columbia	14:1
Iowa	14:1
New Hampshire	14:1
South Dakota	14:1
Massachusetts	14:1
Nebraska	14:1
Connecticut	14:1
Rhode Island	13:1
New York	13:1
Wyoming	13:1
Virginia	13:1
New Jersey	13:1
North Dakota	13:1
Alabama	13:1
Maine	12:1
Vermont	11:1
Note: Data was rounded to the nearest whole number for these estimated averages.	

Discrepancies to Embrace Now

The following are some harsh truths concerning your chosen profession. It is a difficult profession, and it is not for everyone. If you can work past these negatives and focus on the reason you wanted to be a teacher, you will be better prepared to reach your students.

- **Making the difference in the life of even one child makes it all worthwhile.** That sounds great, and may be you will have rewarding moments along the way. The harsh reality is that daily teaching can be monotonous and at times extremely unfulfilling. It can be equated to parenting. What you are doing is extremely important, but that does not mean you will get a lot of gratitude for what you do. For the most part, many people believe that they work daily in their jobs so their taxes can pay your salary.

  If on the other hand, you can hold on to those moments where you have truly reached someone for the first time, you will succeed.

- **The teaching profession has preferable hours.** Many individuals enter the profession thinking it coincides with the hours of their own children's schedules, making it easier. Do not be fooled. Teachers work more than 40 hours each week, just as many other careers. They must come in early and stay later. Much of the time, they must prepare for lessons on their own time. Holidays and vacations may appear to coincide with students, but teachers work many of the days that students have off. Additionally, having the summer off is an appealing concept, but teachers do not actually have three months off for vacation. Extra time is required at the beginning and end of the terms to wrap up and prepare for the next class. Schools also have numerous meeting and seminars that require mandatory attendance.

  As long as you did not become a teacher for the hours, you will be fine. Most other salaried positions require work beyond 40 hours and all through the summer as well.

- **The freedom to move around throughout the day and talk to multiple people makes the day go by quickly.** There is some truth to this. Some days may go by quickly, but mostly because you cannot seem to finish anything you start because of interruptions. On the other hand, there will be days that seem rather slow and tedious. Either way, there is little time to accomplish the little things you may now take for granted, such as eating and going to the bathroom. Today's teachers complain that there is little or no personal time built into daily schedules. Not only does this make planning time difficult, it also makes taking care of yourself a challenge.

  Unfortunately, this is true for most people today, regardless of their chosen profession. The best advice is to take care of yourself. Eat well, sleep as much as you can, and exercise to combat stress.

Prepare for the following

This chapter may seem negative in comparison to what you have learned in college. If you are prepared for some of the harsh realities, there is a better chance you will survive the first year. Additionally, facing facts is easier to do when you know what to expect. The following are a few possibilities you may encounter as a first year high school teacher:

- You will probably have some, if not multiple, students who have been labeled "troubled" or "bad." When scheduling occurs, returning teachers do everything they can to request the students and classes they prefer. New teachers generally get what is left, or the individuals no one wants to work with.

- Your first classroom may be undesirable. It is another issue of seniority. The teachers who have been around the longest will have the best rooms and equipment. You may be stuck with what is left. Quite possibly, you might not have your classroom at all. Use what you are given to the best of your ability. Things change and people leave. If you can weather the storm early on, you will earn the right to choose your own space later on.

- You do not get to teach the subject you are best at. There is a teaching shortage. Because many teachers leave after a short amount of time, you may be slotted in wherever you are needed. It may not be in the grade or subject matter you have prepared for. Be flexible. You will earn the respect of those you work for and with. They may not express it, but you will have a job. That needs to be enough for now. As in most professions, you need to earn your way up the ladder.

- Expect the unexpected. A lot of teaching deals with Murphy's Law. If and when something can go wrong, it probably will. Even the most optimistic person can become depressed when things repeatedly go wrong. Just accept it, and continue to work with what you have. Eventually you will be able to deal with anything you encounter. On that note, if you cannot handle something, do not let your students know. It will make you vulnerable. Keep your emotions in check.

- Do not expect to win over your students or your peers immediately. Earning respect takes time. Do not be afraid to make mistakes or to ask questions. Remain as positive as you can and learn to deal with each scenario as it occurs. You will not earn anyone's respect by whining about your circumstances.

Compensating for crowds

Be prepared. Overcrowding in schools is a nationwide epidemic. According to the Federation for American Immigration Reform (FAIR) report titled, "No Room to Learn: Immigration and School Overcrowding," schools perform better with smaller enrollments. Ideally, high schools should maintain enrollments of between 600 to 900. Despite these findings, 71 percent of secondary schools in the United States have over 1,000 students in attendance. Some of the countries larger cities contain high schools with student bodies numbering 3,000 to 5,000.

Some school districts tend to mislead incoming teachers on the actual teacher-to-student ratio. They do this by using relative math. In other words, they count personnel who assist, but are not actual teachers, such as aides and volunteers. There are numerous reasons for this; some may be financial, while others may have to do with state requirements. Whatever the reasons may be, it is something that new teachers need to be aware of.

The problem of overcrowded classrooms is not limited to big cities, as many people believe. The problem persists in suburban and rural school districts as well. Sometimes the overcrowding in rural and suburban schools is even worse than in the big cities. The fact is there are too few classrooms to adequately house and educate all of the students in the country.

With few exceptions, such as a larger lecture-only class, classes with more students are more challenging to teach. If you are trying to teach a larger number of students with different learning styles and ability levels, particularly if there is a hands-on component to your lesson plan, keeping track of all the students may be difficult.

In many cases, there may be more discipline problems. Additionally, noise may be an issue. It is much more difficult to get 40 teenagers to calm down and get to work than it is 20 students. Problems and noise tend to escalate at an exponential rate. The following are a few ideas on managing an overcrowded classroom:

- Keep a positive attitude. If the students sense you are unhappy with the situation, their attitudes will be negative as well.
- Be prepared and committed to your lesson plan. Try to stay on topic no matter what. If you veer off course, it will be tougher to get everyone back on track.
- Keep your lessons interesting. Captivate your students and encourage them to interact with the lessons, and this will help maintain a cooperative, enjoyable learning environment.

- Teach common courtesy by using it. Do not allow students to interrupt you or each other.
- Keep the noise level at a minimum. Loud noise only makes kids want to get louder.
- Pay attention to room arrangement, making it as open and user-friendly as possible.
- Stay on top of grading papers to reduce your stress. If you get behind with a large number of students, it can be overwhelming to catch up.

Students' ability to focus is another problem that comes with overcrowding, especially if there are one or more students who create distractions. New teachers especially find overcrowding frustrating, because they are in a learning period of their career. Truth be told, even veteran teachers cannot meet the needs of every child in an overcrowded classroom. This does not mean teachers should not, or do not, try; it simply means it is close to impossible to do. When you have an overfull classroom it is even more important to know your students individually in order to have a better chance of helping them.

Asking for help is imperative when you have an overloaded class. Ask if it is possible to get a teacher's aide. Peer tutoring and student pairing may help lighten the load, but try not to rely on this too often. It is not fair to expect students to do this frequently. They may become bitter if they are doing some of the teaching and not having the opportunity to learn something new.

Another product of overcrowded classrooms is insufficient supplies. Many schools are finding that there are not enough textbooks for every student. There are a few ways to handle this situation:

1. Leave the textbooks in the classroom and have students sign them out as needed. This may work in theory, but it can also create another set of problems. Textbooks can disappear. Additionally, it may be difficult for all of the students to get the reading and other assignments completed on time. Subsequently, studying for tests

is an issue, if some of the material is only in the text and all the students do not have copies to take with them prior to the test.

2. Make photocopies of the material that you want the students to read. Have students hole-punch it and keep it in their binders. This way, they have it to study from for future tests and quizzes. An even more effective idea is to blank out some of the words and have them fill the information in during class. It encourages note taking and it becomes a better study aid.

3. Check to see whether your textbooks are available online. Some book companies now offer full copies of their textbooks online. Many of them are even interactive for studying. This is great for multiple reasons. Students will not need to constantly carry 50 or more pounds of books back and forth to school every day, and it will eliminate the "I forgot to take my book home" excuse for not completing the assignment.

Another by-product of overcrowded classrooms may be a shortage of desks. If you find yourself in this situation, hopefully it is only temporary. Talk to the administrative staff to determine whether there are extra desks anywhere in storage or in another teacher's classroom that you can use. If not, find out what you need to do to order additional desks and chairs. In the meantime, find out if there are tables and chairs you can use.

Overcrowding is a stressful issue for both teachers and administrators. The problems that arise due to overcrowding can become major issues. According to teachers surveyed for a report by the National Economics & Social Rights Initiative organization, there is a small increase in school violence with overcrowding because students are harder to control. In 2006, an interim principal in Chicago was fired for refusing to enroll more students in an already overcrowded high school. The new student roster would have pushed classroom sizes to more than 40 students per classroom. Interim Principal Martin McGreal was fired from his position, but he was adamant in saying the extra students he was expected to enroll were too much. The school would have been forced to add a third shift of classes; the shift starting at noon and ending at 6 p.m. Most of the parents applauded McGreal and were pleased he tried to do the right thing for the students. Unfortunately, the school added the third shift due to allowing more enrollments and overcrowded classrooms is still an issue.

Students and teachers sometimes find themselves forced into cramped spaces that were never meant to be classrooms because of overcrowding. Cramped areas plus too many bodies equals health problems. Overcrowding causes more than just the adverse effect on learning — the spread of colds, influenza, skin disorders, and other health issues are more widespread in classrooms that have a large number of students. This also means the teacher is more likely to catch whatever germ happens to be floating around on any given day. Washing your hands as often as possible, exercising, eating right, and reducing stress is the best fight against the germs you will come into contact with daily.

Student overcrowding also affects the bathrooms. Not only does this problem make it harder to keep the bathrooms clean, which causes more germs and health hazards, but it is harder for teachers to allow students to go to the bathroom due to an abundance of people in the building.

In 2008, the Education Department enrollment figures showed some schools in New York were as much as 200 percent over capacity. Many teachers agree overcrowding affects their instructional techniques. Research as far back as 1988 has proven that congested classrooms cause more stress for teachers and it also leads to more teacher absenteeism due to physical sickness and stress. Early burnout is another effect that stuffed classrooms have on teachers, and it is an important point to consider. In a 2008 survey, 76 percent of first-year teachers said that reducing class size would be "a very effective" way of improving teacher quality, and 21 percent said that it would be an "effective" method.

Teachers and students alike often feel overwhelmed and dismayed by the shortage of space and the consequences overcrowding has on learning. Students complained their papers were not checked daily and they did not feel comfortable "taking part in class discussions or special projects." The report also stated that "teachers are deeply disturbed by overcrowding, and staff stress management related to overcrowding." Teachers have also reported overcrowding as the largest threat to safety due to tension and chaos created by sharing a crowded space. The exasperation and frustration teachers experience because of the inability to have good relationships with their students in overcrowded classrooms was another major concern, according to a report by the National Economic & Social Rights Initiative and the Teachers Unite organization.

While overcrowding is a major concern and issue, it is still possible to survive teaching under these conditions. Holding your students' attention is a priority, but once you have that attention you can build a team environment.

All Dressed Up and No Place to Go

Another possible scenario is having no classroom at all. Some individuals have the added challenge of not only having to plan what they need for their lessons, but also having the need to carry it with them as they go. In a time of growing budget constraints, many schools have to find alternatives for dealing with overcrowded classrooms. In prior years, the schools trend was to add trailers or other spaces as a quick fix to the solution of insufficient class space. A less expensive solution is taking its place during these challenging economic times. Instead of adding space, schools are learning how to use the spaces they have to the point of maximum efficiency. They do this by overlapping classroom usage with multiple teachers. Some teachers are deemed "floaters" and do not have a permanent space of their own. There classes take place in different rooms depending on availability.

In these situations, you may be required to share a space with another teacher or staff member. If that happens, be respectful of the other individual. It may be a shock to him as well. If a veteran teacher suddenly has to share a space with you, he may not appreciate it either. Approach the situation accordingly.

The situation is not ideal, to say the least. Hopefully it is just temporary. Either way, you need to adjust and find a way to deal with the situation. Many new teachers are faced with similar circumstances each year. Think about your priorities and go from there.

1. Find a cart. You will need to have a way to transport your supplies. Ask around to find out how to obtain one that can be designated as yours for the remainder of your time as a roaming teacher. If you do not plan for this in the beginning, you risk having someone take your cart for other purposes when you are not around. Supplies in general are coveted in the school environment. Larger, more expensive items, such as carts may be in short supply. You have a valid argument for needing a permanent cart; you just need to find out whom to approach about getting one. Remember, if you are pleasant when you make the request, you will have a better chance of obtaining what you need than if you demand something with an air of entitlement.

2. Locate a safe spot in the building for your personal belongings. There will be times during the day when you cannot pay attention to your cart. Therefore, it is not the best place to store personal items, such as purses, cell phones, and keys. Find a teacher or other staff member you trust and ask if you can have a spot to lock up your personal belongings.

3. Visit and assess the classrooms you will be working in. You will not have the luxury of organizing the furniture to fit your needs. In order to ensure your success, and the success of your class, find a way to work with the environment as is. It does not matter how nice the other teacher is. The person who permanently occupies the space does not want you to reorganize the space to fit your needs.

Getting and staying organized without a classroom

After you obtain the cart, you need to figure out how to get and keep it organized for all of your classes. The following are a few tips for setting it up to suit your needs.

- Procure a lightweight box to use as a filing system. You can purchase a small filing system from any office supply store. If you are short on funds, consider using a milk crate or square plastic tub. Include hanging folders and manila files to organize handouts and other paperwork you will need daily. For security reasons, do not include paperwork on students that should remain private. Find another location for that information — perhaps a locked file drawer allocated by another teacher or support staff member. Another possibility is to carry a lockable briefcase for any materials that may be questionable.

- Obtain a variety of plastic bins with lids in different sizes. You may also want a box of large plastic bags that zip closed. You will need a place for all of your school supplies. Do not assume that you can use the supplies that belong to the teacher who occupies the classroom. Bring everything you could possibly need. The lids and zip enclosures will help secure items in case of an accident. Do not underestimate the possibility of someone bumping into the cart. You will want to make sure all items are secure and organized. Having to pick up items and put them back in the proper bins takes up too much time. Plan accordingly.

- Carry a small first aid kit. Plan for items you would normally keep in your desk to get through the day. These items are for you, not the students. You can always send them to the nurse's office. You, on the other hand, will not have time to go to the nurse's office. Your emergency kit should include anything you might need throughout a typical day. For example it might contain ibuprofen, tissues, hand sanitizer, hand cream, bandages, safety pins, and a needle and thread.

- Be creative. Make the cart yours by decorating with items that pertain to the class. You may not have bulletin boards, but you can still find away to advertise your class. Use the space you have. You may even want to decorate it for the holidays. Some roaming teachers even add flashing colored lights to their carts.

- Above all, maintain a positive attitude and keep your sense of humor. Those two things alone will help you get through the worst of it. If you have the right attitude, you can turn this into a positive experience. For example, you will get more exercise each day than your peers who remain in their classrooms each day.

Other Duties Upon Request

Teaching is beyond a full-time position. It requires a big time commitment, especially when you are first starting out. Plan to work round the clock on lesson plans and grading your first year. Additionally, there may be many other tasks and responsibilities that affect your time as well. There are four primary categories: school-day tasks, after school requirements, extracurricular activities, and meetings. Here are some of the time constraint factors you may not have considered:

School-day tasks

As a teacher, you expect to spend hours planning lessons and grading work. As a new high school teacher, you probably be teaching five or six classes a day. You are prepared for that. You may not realize, however, that the remaining unscheduled hours are not free planning time. Especially in the current economic climate, with huge school budget cuts, you will be expected to handle a number of other responsibilities. These "as needed" tasks could include:

- **Covering other teachers' classes**
  It is not always easy to get substitutes at the last minute for every class. If a class does not have a scheduled substitute, other teachers will cover during the periods they have open on their schedules. Just remember to have a good attitude and do the best you can. At some point, that teacher may be covering for you some day.

- **Study hall**
  You will probably not be sitting in an empty room during any of your class-free periods. Study halls need monitoring teachers. The

good news is if you have a good group of students, you may be able to get some work done.

- **Clerical jobs**
  All schools require a great deal of paperwork. Even if your school has multiple people in clerical positions, on occasion, you will be expected to copy, collate, staple, and file. You may even need to answer phones or deliver messages. Everyone helps out and the sooner you accept it, the easier it will be.

- **Hallway monitor**
  Some teachers are given hallway or school perimeter detail. In other words, you have to make sure no one is in the wrong place at the wrong time, violating any rules. Since you are dealing with high school students, this can be a challenge. You may have to make sure students get back to class. You may need to break up fights and give out detention. In worse case scenarios, just as drug and weapon infractions, you may even call for law enforcement back up. Whatever the situation, take it seriously. It may seem like babysitting, but it is really security detail. As such, it is very important, so do not stand around talking to other teachers and students — pay attention and do a good job.

- **Cafeteria coverage**
  Cafeteria detail is similar to hallway and parking lot monitoring in that you are really monitoring the safety of the students. Hopefully, the biggest concerns will be students cutting in line. Nonetheless, pay attention. It may seem like an annoying task, but it is still important.

After-school requirements

There may be times you are asked to stay after school to monitor students as well. Some of these items, like detention, may be on a rotating basis. Others may just go to the first available person. As the new man on the totem pole, you will likely be assigned. Take it all in stride. Everything you do earns you experience, and you will not be the new person forever.

- **Detention**
  Detention is generally not anyone's favorite job. It may require you to come in early or stay late. Additionally, you may be dealing with an unruly group of kids. Take it for what it is and work through it. No assignment lasts forever. Some school districts keep students in line with a scheduled work program. For certain infractions or acquiring too many detentions, the students are required to come in on Saturday mornings to clean the school bathrooms.

- **Test proctoring**
  Since you are teaching at a high school, there will be times when you are asked to be a test proctor. Depending on the size and location of your school, you may be asked to proctor on multiple dates for PSATs, SATs, or ACTs. This can involve anything from checking IDs to sitting in the testing rooms watching the students take the test. On the plus side, you may be paid for your time.

- **Tutoring**
  There are different types of tutoring. There are some instances where you will stay late to run study groups for an upcoming test. There are other times where you may take on an additional assignment as a paid tutor.

Extracurricular activities

Depending on the type and size of your high school, there will undoubtedly be a number of extracurricular activities. Some people volunteer to lead these groups because of a past history in the activity. Many others end up being assigned because no one else would do it. First-year teachers are frequently assigned these responsibilities. It does not matter that you feel completely overwhelmed and snowed under with paperwork. You can try to say you are still trying to get acclimated to the job, but it will not work. Many others before you have tried unsuccessfully. Rather than try to avoid the inevitable, show that you are flexible and willing to be a team player — it will benefit you in the long run.

- **Club adviser**
  If there is an activity you would like to be involved in from personal experience or interest, look into that first. If there is an opening, the school would love to have you share your experience. If not, you will probably be targeted for either a new group or one that no one wants. Student groups are generally not allowed to organize without an adult sponsor. In many schools, students can start a club with as few as five individuals as long as they find a teacher to sponsor the group and attend the meetings. Since you are new, students may approach you to sponsor their new group.

"Some club advisors get compensated, but others do not in public school. It's usually a union issue. When one teacher asked for compensation, she was told to take it up with the union. To be honest, unless you are the football coach or wrestling coach, the financial reward is quite slim. Teachers at our school do not usually get involved with these activities for the money."

— Kathy Heisler, International Baccalaureate program coordinator, Cumberland Valley High School

- **Sporting event assistance**
  Most schools have a wide array of sports teams. In addition to coaching, there are any number of other tasks that need volunteers. Some schools pay teachers a small amount for these tasks. Others do not. These responsibilities include keeping scorebooks

and other stats, running scoreboards, helping in concession stands, working at fundraisers, and being an announcer.

- **Other social events**
  In addition to clubs and sports, there are social endeavors that require teacher presence. School dances need chaperones. There may be talent shows and plays with faculty members at some schools. Some schools host fun events, such as bingo or casino night, and may recruit teacher helpers.

CASE STUDY: THE REWARDS OF COACHING

Jennifer Mulhollen
Itinerant Learning Support Teacher
and Softball Coach
Cumberland Valley School District

Jen Mulhollen is in her sixth year of teaching and her second year as a high school softball coach. She graduated from Shippensburg University with a bachelor's degree in education and a minor in psychology.

Venturing out into the real world, getting your first "real" job teaching is an experience that can't be topped. When you take this plunge it is the first real sign that you are grown up and leaving some of the things of your youth behind. It is exciting and terrifying at the same time. When I got my first real teaching job and had to come to the realization that I am not able to play fast pitch softball anymore (competitively anyway) it hit me like a brick. Is there a way to be able to be involved in what you love and live your adult life? Absolutely! Coaching, for me, was the next logical step in order to not give up that part of me. I was so excited when I found out that they were looking for a softball coach to help out with the high school program that I jumped right in; put absolutely no thought into it.

Jumping right into a coaching experience is not something that should be taken lightly. When you are in your first few years of teaching everything is new. All of your work is new, you have nothing already prepared which means you spend hours upon hours doing lesson plans and writing tests and grading and just getting acclimated to the teaching profession. When you take on an extracurricular activity like coaching this takes up a ton of time. Don't get me wrong, I love teaching and I love coaching but adding this extra responsibility to your schedule is tiring, especially when you coach teenagers!

I also teach middle school, which involves a lot of drama. High school students are a totally different breed. One thing that I noticed is that the teenagers I coach want to do extremely well on the field and in the classroom. They are incredibly focused. They will do whatever they need to do in order to get as much playing time as possible, which not only includes doing well at practice but also doing well in the classroom. If they don't keep up their grades then they don't get to play, so it all goes hand in hand.

I had a few players who were so focused on their schoolwork after practice that they would be up all hours of the night in order to continue to do well in school. For a lot of students they actually do better in school when the season is in, it forces students to do their work when they have the time. These students are so focused on what it is that they want that they do whatever it takes to get it and it shows both in the classroom and on the field. It is incredibly refreshing to work with students who want to do their best in everything that they do.

Meetings

Your presence may also be requested at numerous meetings. Some may be more important than others. Some you absolutely must attend. If you are uncertain, ask a colleague.

- **Staff and Department Meetings**
  If the school is having a staff meeting, you must attend. There may be a policy change or you might be celebrating someone's retirement. Either way, if they call it a staff meeting, you should go. Department meetings will be with the chairperson of your department and other staff members who teach in your department. These are also important. They will concern department

goals, textbooks, materials, budgets for supplies, and other program specific information.

- **PTO/PTA and school board**
  School-related meetings may require your presence as a representative of the staff. Additionally, you may find they are discussing a topic pertinent to your job or a major change at the school.

Chapter 12

Final Advice

Teaching is a stressful, yet incredibly rewarding career. No two days will be exactly alike and you will continue to grow and learn as a teacher and as a person along with your students as you continue teaching. This chapter includes some final thoughts on professional development, tips on avoiding rookie mistakes, and stress reduction techniques to help you cope when things go wrong.

Professional Development

You have spent years in school preparing to teach. You are finally working in your chosen profession and it is going to take a while to get into a routine. That is all you have to concentrate on this year, correct? Not exactly. As soon as you start teaching, you need to start thinking ahead for what you need to do to plan your professional development. Every state has its own specific guidelines for teacher professional development. Some states require you to pile on credits in the first few year of teaching.

There is also a variety in the time frame you are expected to complete the development in. For example, in Pennsylvania, when a teacher receives his Level I teaching certificate, he will have six years to begin using that certificate. If he doesn't begin teaching on that certificate for three years, that time does not count toward time used on the certificate. When a teacher begins teaching on his Level I certificate, he will have six years to apply for his Level

II certificate. He can apply for his Level II certificate once he meets the minimum of three years teaching on that certificate and his attainment of 24 post-baccalaureate credits. For general teaching, there is not a specific time frame required to obtain your master's degree.

Additionally, there may be a time component. For example, in Pennsylvania, educators must meet 180 hours every five years to keep their certificate active. Any way you look at it, it is additional school you will have to attend and it is extra time you have to allocate.

Rather than become overwhelmed from waiting too long, check out your state's criteria right away. If you start scheduling it now, in smaller increments, it will be easier to handle. There are a few options for professional development courses. They are:

- **In-service training.** The good news is it can count towards professional development requirements. The bad news is you will not have time for grading, organizing, and lesson planning on those extra days.

- **Classes on the weekends.** Depending on the length of the class, you could take a class that lasts a couple of hours or longer. May seem like a convenient option, until you have grading that you cannot get done any other time.

- **Classes on the Internet.** These courses do not require you to leave home, which is a big plus. If you schedule them during the school year, you could be adding extra stress.

- **Summer classes.** Some people want to leave their summers for fun vacations or spending time with their families. That is understandable. Nonetheless, summer is the easiest time to get professional development completed and out of the way.

Rookie Mistakes

As a new teacher, you will make rookie mistakes. Although you will not always have control of the situation all of the time, you can try to avoid some common mistakes made by new teachers. The following are a few suggestions to keep you out of trouble.

1. Do not try to bribe your class with treats and prizes. They will get used to this and it will end up costing you a lot of money.
2. Do not let the boundary slip between teacher and student. You are not their friend. If you forget this, it could end up costing you more than a few problems.
3. Set class rules and stick to them. If you do not follow through, you will lose credibility.
4. Do not let your students intimidate you. You are the teacher. You make the rules.
5. Do not worry about what the students think about you. Do your job.
6. Always think before you speak. You do not need to be misinterpreted right away.
7. Look at yourself before you teach. Something in your teeth or on your clothes will have the class laughing at you all day.
8. Always have emergency back-up lesson plans.
9. Take your lunch break and do not let anyone intrude on it.
10. Do not hesitate to ask for help.

CASE STUDY: I SURVIVED FIVE YEARS OF TEACHING HIGH SCHOOL

Rachele Dominick
English Teacher
Cumberland Valley High School
Mechanicsburg, PA

Rachele Dominick spent her first five years of teaching English at Cumberland Valley High School. Cumberland Valley High School (CV) is a coeducational public high school founded in 1954. It is located in Mechanicsburg, Cumberland County, Pennsylvania. This area is suburban and is located 15 miles west of Pennsylvania's capital city Harrisburg. It is the 16th largest public high school in the state. Here are here reflections on her first five years of teaching at the high school level:

On becoming a teacher:

I have always enjoyed reading and writing. I had originally planned on becoming a reporter when I entered college, but soon realized the competitive nature of that field, and decided it would be better for me to be in the classroom. I soon realized that it was meant to be! When I decided to teach, I knew I wanted to teach advanced, higher level types of learners. My forte is discussing complex, abstract ideas. After three years of teaching English, I got the opportunity to teach Advance Placement (AP) English and I love it. My ultimate goal is to teach at the college level, so AP English is the closest thing for me right now.

I remember being in high school and thinking, "If I am ever a teacher, I would do it this way or that way." But as an adult now on the other end of things, sometimes situations have more involvement than students can see at the time. The best that you can do is to always put the students' learning first, and to keep their interests at heart.

As an English teacher, I must say that the best training was in taking as many English classes in college as I could. Yes, the education courses were helpful theory-wise, but my advice is to gain as much content knowledge as possible.

I highly recommend student teaching. Student teaching was the best preparation. Everything studied prior to this experience was theory. Theory is important, but sometimes theory cannot solve real issues in the classroom. Practice is the fastest teacher.

I finished up my degree as a fall graduate, meaning that I finished in December. I thought about becoming a substitute, but decided instead to use the semester looking for jobs and finding the perfect fit. It worked, because a position was opening in CV for the following fall term. This has been a great place to work.

Remember that the interview is as much for you as it is for the district. Ask questions and make sure that it is the right fit for you. My current job was my third interview, and I knew when I left that it was different from the first two and that it would be a place where I would feel at home.

On preparing the classroom:

One of the most important things for me to establish right away is a comfortable classroom atmosphere. When students know that they are safe and that their opinions are appreciated, they will be more willing to take risks in discussions, therefore gaining more intellectual freedom.

In reference to setting up your classroom, I suggest creating an atmosphere that is welcoming. Because I have an English classroom, I set up my desks in a circular formation, so that it is productive for discussion. I also have a corner with a sofa and chair so that students can come in and read comfortably. Use colors and keep it neat and organized. People generally feel more comfortable when their surroundings are clean.

There is an old adage that says, “Don’t smile until Christmas.” I suppose this is meant to establish a type of fear that results in good behavior. I don’t believe this. I smile on the first day. I let the students know that I am a person, that I have a personality, and that class can be enjoyable. Generally, if you show respect and a level of trust toward the students, they will answer in the same manner.

I really like working with this age group, especially the mature AP students. My advice would be to tailor instruction to the classroom personality as a whole. Get to know the class, and how they work together. No class is now — or ever will be — the same so don’t try to repeat verbatim a lesson to another group of students. Make your personality fit with the class and to create a mutual respect.

In reference to working with parents:

Usually, parents and teachers have the same goal in mind: achievement of the student. Keep this in mind.

On the subject of lesson plans:

At Cumberland Valley, we do not need to follow a specific format, so I use what works for me. I think that it is important to have the end result in mind and to create a general plan for what the assessment will be at the end of the unit. Lesson plans should work to reach the end result. One thing that I have noticed is that high school students are not prone to take notes unless they are prompted. To compensate, I type up discussion points or questions that I would like to cover that day. Then students can take notes on the sheet with the questions. This keeps the discussion on track, lays out what they should know regarding the reading, and sends out the message that it is time to write. Also, if you do not get to all of the questions in class, you can either assign the rest for homework or announce that all of the questions are eligible for a test.

And on the subject of the test – it takes a very long time to write up a test for the very first time. I didn't expect that.

What I have learned and would pass on to any new high school teachers:

Take things one day at a time. It is easy to become overwhelmed in this profession, especially during the first year when everything is new. As long as you are one day ahead of the students, and have prepared well for the day at hand, you will be great.

Stress Reduction Techniques

Many of the realities surrounding teaching can be stressful and unpleasant. The bottom line is that life is stressful regardless of the job you take. The important thing is to have a job you enjoy. The following are a few tips for managing your stress when you are having a bad day:

1. **Talk a walk.** If things are not going well during the day and you can find a way to walk around the building during a break, do it. If you cannot find the time during the day, take a walk or go to a gym as soon as you leave work. If you are tempted to go home first, you may be too tired to go out. If you make the time to do something for yourself before you get home, you will be less stressed and less tired. The exercise will re-energize you, enabling you to grade papers and prepare the next day's lesson.

2. **Call a friend.** Sometimes, a little venting can go a long way. Get your feelings out and then move on. To make sure you do not fall into a pattern of whining, set a kitchen timer for five to ten minutes. When the timer goes off, you are done venting and it is time to talk about something else.

3. **Get enough sleep.** After school, take breaks for a specific amount of time, such as walking for an hour. Make a schedule for getting your evening work done, so you are not up to late. You will be more stressed the next day if you did not get enough sleep.

4. **Take a bath.** There is something magical about the healing powers of a hot bath. Give yourself some time to unwind.

5. **Do some yoga.** Yoga and other forms of meditation can help relieve stress. Take a class or put in a DVD at home.

6. **Spend some time outside.** If the weather is nice, work in the garden or sit on a porch swing. If it is winter, take a brisk walk or build a snowman.

7. **Watch a movie.** Watching television or movies can be a great escape in moderation. Be sure you plan your time accordingly so that you do not end up working late because of it.

8. **Play.** Find someone to laugh with, be it a significant other, a child, or a pet. Do something silly and fun. Nothing relieves stress like laughter.

9. **Listen to music.** Pick music that soothes you. It is different for everyone. For some people it might be jazz, for others it might be country. Whatever you enjoy, turn it up and lose yourself in the music.

10. **Plan a getaway.** When you have a weekend that is not too full, find a way to give yourself a mini-vacation. Drive to the beach or visit a friend. Stay at home and turn off your phone and read all weekend. Whatever the plan is, make it just for you.

For effective stress relief, you must be able to disconnect yourself from what is causing you stress. Think it through and then put it aside for as long as you can reasonably allow. Maybe it is 20 minutes or maybe it is an entire weekend. Remember, you will be a better teacher when you are in a good frame of mind. Make sure to make time for yourself.

As a new teacher, you will truly be tested. You will encounter values and beliefs that shock you. You will hear complaints about you from students and parents. You will also hear statements that unnerve you. One phrase in particular comes to mind: "those who can, do; those who can't, teach." Anyone in the field of education realizes what a ridiculous statement that really is. Learn to develop a thick skin and remember why you wanted to be a teacher to begin with. Additionally, know that you may be making a very important positive impact on a student in a way you may never even know about.

CASE STUDY: WHAT TEACHING MEANS TO ME

Ruth H. Bortolan
Retired Teacher
South Windsor, CT

Ruth Bortolan is recently retired after teaching and mentoring in Connecticut for more than 40 years. She holds a bachelor's of science degree and a master's degree. Over the years, she worked on school certification evaluation committees, state education curriculum committees, and local teacher mentoring programs. She was also published in the New England Celebration of Excellence Project magazine. She has many memories and stories from her years of teaching. In her opinion, this particular story provides an excellent example of what she loved about teaching and why new teachers should never take for granted the impact they make on their students.

When I attended St. Joseph College, I took a child development course. The teacher, Sister Mary de Lourdes, taught all of her college prep teachers that the most important thing a teacher can do is greet each student with an honest positive comment each and every day. It isn't difficult to find something nice to say even something as simple as, "you have a nice smile today," or "that's a cool new hairstyle." I remembered this advice when I became a teacher, and I really tried to implement it often.

During my second year of teaching, I was monitoring a study hall that primarily consisted of ninth-grade students discussing the fact that they would quit school as soon as they turned 16. I remember one boy in particular who was starved for attention and acting out negatively in order to get someone to notice him. One day, I politely asked him to move his seat since he was bothering the students near him. He moved to a seat near the window and proceeded to make a hangman's noose out of the cord hanging from the window shade. He then came up to me and announced that he had made the noose especially for me. I told him that I was sorry to have to give him a "pink" pass, the third one from me in about a week. At that time, three pink passes meant he would get two weeks suspension from school. He took the pass and left the room. I did not really think anything more about it.

A few weeks later, I was wrapping things up to leave my job at that school. I was getting married to a man who was in the military, and we were being transferred to another state. The staff at the school had thrown me a bridal shower that afternoon, and I was one of the last people out of the building that day.

It was snowing and my car was the only one in the front parking lot. As I approached my car, I remember feeling frightened because the boy who had made me the hangman's noose was standing there. Instead of showing my fear, I kept on walking, said "hello," and asked him how he was doing and why he was there. He told me he had heard that I was leaving the school, so he had waiting outside in the cold and snow to talk to me before I left. He wanted to tell me that I was the only teacher who had ever been nice to him, and he wanted to thank me. I surely learned something that day: never underestimate the power of your words or how you treat people.

I was a new bride off to live my life. I have since forgotten the boy's name, but over the years I have often wondered how he made out in life. It is amazing how many times over the years I have thought of him. When I returned to teaching (I taught for 30 more years), I always remembered to say something nice to each student as often as I could. This made my teaching job easy and joyful, because the students always treated me the way I treated them.

Treating people well is important at any level, but as a first year teacher it can help you establish positive relationships that will help you for years. First year teachers in any new position, whether they have experience or not, have tons of work to do. Build a rapport with your students and ask them for help with minor tasks, like setting up bulletin boards. It will help you get to know them, and it will give them a chance to feel helpful. This can build a relationship that is supportive for both of you.

Conclusion

"Teaching is the profession that teaches all the other professions."

— Author Unknown

Teaching is never going to be the easiest career, but it is never more difficult than it is during your first year. No matter how well you did in school or in a previous career, you will never be completely prepared for what you will encounter as an educator. Heed the advice of the teachers who came before you. Listen to the tips written by the veteran teachers in this book. Find a mentor and listen to everything they tell you. It is a difficult job, but it is also incredibly rewarding if you stick with it. Hopefully, this book will help you navigate some of the most common pitfalls new teachers face each year. Before you know it, you will be able to share your own wisdom with new teachers just getting started.

Everyone has his or her own reasons for getting into the teaching profession. Those who stay the course are those who get into for the right reasons. As the quote implies – yours is the profession responsible for training all others. Every day you will encounter students at various stages of maturity, growth, and development. They are only beginning their own personal journeys. Be passionate about what you do, for any one of these young minds may be responsible for great things some day. Think how rewarding it will be for you to be able to say, "I was that person's teacher."

Bibliography

"12 Tips for Substitute Teachers." *Why Teach?* Web. 12 Nov. 2009. <**www.whyteach.wordpress.com/2008/04/24/12-tips-for-substitute-teachers**>.

"2008 - 2009 Salary Survey." NACST - *National Association of Catholic School Teachers.* Web. 12 Nov. 2009. <**www.nacst.com**>.

"Military School Web site." *Military school: education academies schools, boarding school, top private boy military schools, boot camp information for the cadet and parents.* Web. 08 Dec. 2009. <**www.military-school.org**>.

"AFT - Teacher Salary - Teacher Salaries - Teachers Salary - Teachers Pay - Teacher Pay." *AFT - American Federation of Teachers.* Web. 11 Nov. 2009. <**www.aft.org/salary/**>.

"Annual Data Report - National Catholic Educational Association." *Home Page - National Catholic Educational Association.* Web. 08 Dec. 2009. <**www.ncea.org/news/AnnualDataReport.asp#schools09**>.

American Federation of Teachers. AFT. Web. 7 Nov. 2009. <**www.aft.org/about**>.

"Become a Substitute Teacher." *Teacher World - Education for Teachers and Administrators.* Web. 25 Nov. 2009. <**www.teacher-world.com/substitute-teacher.html**>.

Become a Teacher - *Top Teacher Training Resource.* Web. 10 Oct. 2009. <**www.becomeateacher.info/Certification-Requirements.asp**>.

"Best High Schools: Gold Medal List." *US News and World Report.* USNews.com, 4 Dec. 2008. Web. 14 Nov. 2009. <**www.usnews.com/articles/education/high-schools/2008/12/04/best-high-schools-gold-medal-list.html**>.

Burell, Clay. "Data for the Teacher Union Bashers (including Bill Maher and Arianna Huffington) |." *Education | Change.org.* Web. 14 Nov. 2009. <**www.education.change.org/blog/view/data_for_the_teacher_union_bashers_including_bill_maher_and_arianna_huffington**>.

"CAPE | Private School Facts." *CAPE | Council for American Private Education.* Web. 01 Mar. 2010. <**www.capenet.org/facts.html**>.

Castro, Antonio J., and Michelle Bauml. "Why now? Factors associated with choosing teaching as a second career and their implications for teacher education programs." Publication Education Quarterly (2009). The Free Library by Farlex. Web. 10 Feb. 2010. <www.thefreelibrary.com/Why+now%3F+Factors+associated+with+choosing+teaching+as+a+second+career...-a0210591618>.

Davidson, Jan, Bob Davidson, and Laura Vanderkam. *Genius Denied How to Stop Wasting Our Brightest Young Minds.* New York: Simon & Schuster, 2004. Web. 13 Nov. 2009. <**www.geniusdenied.com**>.

"Developing a Teaching Resume & Cover Letter :: :: A to Z Teacher Stuff." *A to Z Teacher Stuff For Teachers FREE online lesson plans, lesson plan ideas and activities, thematic units, printables, themes, teaching tips, articles, and educational resources.* Web. 25 Nov. 2009. <**www.atozteacherstuff.com/pages/1876.shtml**>.

Dillon, Sam. "High Schools to Offer Plans to Graduate 2 Years Early." *The New York Times.* TimesPeople, 17 Feb. 2010. Web. 10 Mar. 2010. <**www.nytimes.com/2010/02/18/education/18educ.html?hp**>.

Dumont, Deborah. "Deborah Dumont: Students at Charter High Schools More to Likely to Graduate College." *Breaking News and Opinion on The Huffington Post.* 22 Feb. 2010. Web. 04 Mar. 2010. <**www.huffingtonpost.com/deborah-dumont/students-at-charter-high_b_471991.html**>.

"Education - Secondary Education." *The World Bank.* Web. 25 Oct. 2009. <**http://web.worldbank.org/WBSITE/EXTERNAL/TOPICS/EXTEDUCATION/0,,contentMDK:20521252~menuPK:738179~pagePK:148956~piPK:216618~theSitePK:282386,00.html**>.

"Education Quotes | Education Quotations | Education Sayings |." *Wisdom Quotes.* Web. 12 Nov. 2009. <**www.wisdomquotes.com/cat_education.html**>.

"Education Resource Organizations Directory (EROD)." *Wdcrobcolp01.ed.gov.* Web. 14 Oct. 2009. <**http://wdcrobcolp01.ed.gov/Programs/EROD/org_list.cfm?category_cd=SEA**>.

"Education World." *Education World.* Web. 15 Nov. 2009. <**www.education-world.com/a_curr/curr263.shtml**>.

"Elementary & Secondary Pupil/teacher Ratio by State. Definition, Graph and Map." *StateMaster - US Statistics, State Comparisons.* Web. 13 Apr. 2010. <**www.statemaster.com/graph/edu_ele_sec_pup_rat-elementary-secondary-pupil-teacher-ratio**>.

"FAQs." *US Charter Schools Home.* Web. 07 Dec. 2009. <**www.uscharterschools.org/pub/uscs_docs/o/faq.html#3**>.

"Fast Facts." *National Center for Education Statistics (NCES) Home Page, a part of the U.S. Department of Education.* Web. 12 Nov. 2009. <**www.nces.ed.gov/fastfacts/display.asp?id=28**>.

"Format Teacher Resume, Teacher Resume Sample, Teacher Resumes, CV Resume, Educational Resume." *Sample Resumes, Free Sample Resume, Resume Writing Examples.* Web. 25 Nov. 2009. <**www.bestsampleresume.com/teachers-resumes.html**>.

GreatSchools - Public and Private School Ratings, Reviews and Parent Community. Web. 24 Nov. 2009. <**www.greatschools.net**>.

"High School Lesson Plans." *Georgia Educational Technology Training Center.* Web. 15 Nov. 2009. <**http://edtech.kennesaw.edu/intech/hslessonplans.htm**>.

High Schools - public high schools and private high schools. Web. 25 Nov. 2009. <**www.high-schools.com**>.

"Inspiring Teachers - Tips - Dealing with Difficult Parents - Empowering Educators Around the World - classroom resources, tips, articles, newsletter, books, webinars, & free web pages." *Inspiring Teachers - Home - Empowering Educators Around the World - classroom resources, tips, articles, newsletter, books, webinars, & free web pages.* Web. 01 Feb. 2010. <**www.inspiringteachers.com/classroom_resources/tips/parent_communication/dealing_with_difficult_parents.html**>.

Job interviews. Free interview questions and answers and job interview tips. Web. 08 Nov. 2009. <**www.best-job-interview.com**>.

Kelley, W. Michael. *Rookie Teaching for Dummies.* New York: For Dummies, 2003. Print.

Kelly, Melissa. "Rubrics - How to Make Grading Easier - Rubrics." *Secondary School Education - Education and Teaching.* Web. 06 Feb. 2010. <**www.712educators.about.com/cs/rubrics/a/rubrics.htm**>.

Lambert, Lisa. "Half of Teachers Quit in 5 Years." *The Washington Post* [Washington, DC] 9 May 2006. Web. 15 Nov. 2009. <**www.washingtonpost.com/wp-dyn/content/article/2006/05/08/AR2006050801344.html**>.

"Learnng Styles Take Your Test." *Learning Styles - Take Learning Styles Test.* LdPride. Web. 07 Feb. 2010. <**www.ldpride.net/learningstyles.MI.htm#types%20of%20Multiple%20Intelligence**>.

LE ROSEY: A Prestigious International Boarding School in Switzerland. Web. 10 Nov. 2009. <**www.rosey.ch/en/htmlRosey/histoire.html**>.

"Lesson Plans." *Teachers Network.* Web. 14 Nov. 2009. <**www.teachersnetwork.org/lessonplans**>.

Lorenz, Kate. "CNN.com - Tricks to remembering names - Jul 22, 2005." *CNN.com - Breaking News, U.S., World, Weather, Entertainment & Video News.* CNN, 22 July 2005. Web. 05 Dec. 2009. <**www.cnn.com/2005/US/Careers/07/22/names**>.

Mauro, Terri. "What Is a 504 Plan?" *Parenting Special Needs Children.* About.com. Web. 25 Nov. 2009. <**www.specialchildren.about.com/od/504s/f/504faq1.htm**>.

Mentor: Expanding the world of quality mentoring. Web. 13 Nov. 2009. <**www.mentoring.org/take_action/advocate_for_mentoring/background_checks/legislative_history**>.

National Association of School Nurses. Web. 08 Dec. 2009. <**www.nasn.org**>.

National Education Association. NEA. Web. 5 Nov. 2009. <**www.nea.org/home/1704.htm**>.

"No Room To Learn: Immigration and School Overcrowding." *The Federation for American Immigration Reform (FAIR):*. Web. 13 Apr. 2010. <**www.fairus.org/site/PageServer?pagename=research_research438f**>.

Novak, Lauren. "More turn to teaching as a second career." *Adelaide Now.* The Advertiser, 27 Nov. 2009. Web. 10 Feb. 2010. <**www.adelaidenow.com.au/news/in-depth/more-turn-to-teaching-as-a-second-career/story-fn3o6nna-1225803210915**>.

Nutt, Amy. "The Importance of Post Secondary Education in Furthering Your Career." *Ezine Articles (R).* Ezine, 25 June 2007. Web. 25 Oct. 2009. <**www.ezinearticles.com/?The-Importance-of-Post-Secondary-Education-in-Furthering-Your-Career&id=620729**>.

"Online High Schools - What is Cyber School?" *Online High Schools - Home.* Web. 07 Dec. 2009. <**www.cyberhighschools.com/What_is_Cyber_School_.html**>.

Palleschi, Amanda. "Mid-career Professionals Head Back to Classrooms." *The Patriot News* [Harrisburg, PA] 12 Oct. 2009. Web. 12 Oct. 2009. <**www.pennlive.com**>.

Schlechter, Kira L. "Pennsylvania private schools' downturn expected to continue." *The Patriot News* [Harrisburg, PA] 22 Sept. 2009. *All Business.* Web. 10 Oct. 2009. <**www.allbusiness.com/education-training/education-systems-institutions/13030472-1.html**>.

Pennsylvania State Education Association. PSEA. Web. 7 Nov. 2009. <**www.psea.org/default.aspx**>.

"Private Schools and Boarding Schools Search Find Private Schools with Peterson's." *Search for Colleges and Universities, Graduate Schools, Online Degree, Private Schools - Peterson's.* Web. 06 Dec. 2009. <**www.petersons.com/pschools/code/StateCtryResult.asp?sponsor=1&from=psector**>.

"Pros and Cons of Different Types of Schooling." *Gifted Kids - Gifted Children - IQ - IQ Tests - Intelligence Tests - Family Education.* Web. 07 Dec. 2009. <**www.extremeintellect.com/08EDUCATION/prosconsschooltypes.htm**>.

"Public and private elementary and secondary teachers, enrollment, and pupil/teacher ratios: Selected years, fall 1955 through fall 2017." *National Center for Education Statistics (NCES) Home Page, a part of the U.S. Department of Edu-*

cation. Web. 12 Nov. 2009. <**www.nces.ed.gov/programs/digest/d08/tables/dt08_064.asp**>.

Public Schools & Private Schools - Local School Directory. Web. 14 Nov. 2009. <**www.localschooldirectory.com**>.

Public School Review - Profiles of USA Public Schools. Web. 07 Dec. 2009. <**www.publicschoolreview.com**>.

"Quotations on Teaching, Learning, and Education." *The National Teaching & Learning Forum.* Web. 12 Nov. 2009. <**www.ntlf.com/html/lib/quotes.htm**>.

"Quotes on Education." *Lock Haven University of Pennsylvania.* Web. 13 Nov. 2009. <**www.lhup.edu/~dsimanek/eduquote.htm**>.

"Resources: 25 Useful Lesson Plan Links | Teaching Tips." *Teaching Tips.com - Online Teacher Certificates - Become a Teacher.* Web. 30 Oct. 2009. <**www.teachingtips.com/library/education-as-a-career-faqs/resources-25-useful-lesson-plan-links**>.

"Resources for School Counselors." *American Counseling Association.* Web. 07 Dec. 2009. <**www.counseling.org/PublicPolicy/TP/ResourcesForSchool-Counselors/CT2.aspx**>.

"Secondary School Teachers, Except Special and Vocational Education." *U.S. Bureau of Labor Statistics.* Web. 15 Nov. 2009. <**www.bls.gov/oes/2008/may/oes252031.htm#msa**>.

"Should You Worry About School Violence?" *KidsHealth - the Web's most visited site about children's health.* Web. 07 Dec. 2009. <**www.kidshealth.org/teen/school_jobs/bullying/school_violence.html**>.

Sprick, Randall S. Discipline in the Secondary *Classroom: a Positive Approach to Behavior Management.* Second ed. San Francisco: Jossey-Bass, 2006. Print.

Teacher Certification Map | Become a Teacher. Web. 27 Feb. 2010. <**www.certificationmap.com**>.

"Teacher Quotes, Teaching Sayings, Quotations about Teachers." *The Quote Garden - Quotes, Sayings, Quotations, Verses.* Web. 12 Nov. 2009. <**www.quotegarden.com/teachers.html**>.

"Teacher Resume and Cover Letter Examples." *A Resumes for Teachers.* Web. 24 Nov. 2009. <**www.resumes-for-teachers.com/teacher-resume-examples.htm**>.

Teacher Retention and Attrition Information, Questions and Answers. Web. 25 Nov. 2009. <**www.retainingteachers.com**>.

"Teacher Salaries By State | Average Salaries For Teachers | Beginning Salaries For Teachers | Teacher Raises | TeacherPortal.com." *Teacher Training and Teaching Resources | Teacher Portal.* Web. 12 Nov. 2009. <**www.teacherportal.com/teacher-salaries-by-state**>.

"Teacher Salary - Average Teacher Salaries - PayScale." *PayScale - Salary Comparison, Salary Survey, Wages.* Web. 12 Nov. 2009. <**www.payscale.com/research/US/All_K-12_Teachers/Salary**>.

"Teacher Salary Breakdown of Data." *Teacher Salary - How to find more and make more.* Web. 12 Nov. 2009. <**www.teachersalaryinfo.com/teacher-salary-data.html**>.

"Teacher Salary Secrets Revealed | Compare Teacher Salaries On All Education Schools." *All Education Schools - Teaching Degree & Teaching Credential Resources | Find Accredited Online Teacher Training Programs.* Web. 10 Nov. 2009. <**www.alleducationschools.com/faqs/teacher-salary.php**>.

"Teachers and teaching quotes." *Find the famous quotes you need, ThinkExist.com Quotations.* Web. 12 Nov. 2009. <**http://thinkexist.com/quotations/teachers_and_teaching/2.html**>.

"Teaching quotations, Teacher quotations, teacher quotes, teaching quotes --MAY 2003 from Motivating Moments. Motivational quotes, inspirational quotes, positive quotes and quotations." *Motivational Quotes, motivation quotes, positive quotes, Motivational Quotations, from Motivating Moments.* Web. 12 Nov. 2009. <**www.motivateus.com/teach25.htm**>.

Lavoie, Rick. "The Teacher's Role in Home/School Communication: Everybody Wins." *LD OnLine.* Web. 13 Nov. 2009. <**www.ldonline.org/article/28021**>.

"Tips/Student Teaching." *A to Z Teacher Stuff For Teachers FREE online lesson plans, lesson plan ideas and activities, thematic units, printables, themes, teaching tips, articles, and educational resources.* Web. 12 Nov. 2009. <**www.atozteacherstuff.com/Tips/Student_Teaching**>.

"Undergraduate Degree Programs: General Education in the Curriculum." *University Bulletin: Undergraduate Degree Programs.* "What is General Education?" Web. 8 Nov. 2009. <**www.bulletins.psu.edu/bulletins/bluebook/general_education.cfm?section=generalEd1**>.

"United States - Secondary Education." Web. 12 Nov. 2009. <**http://education.stateuniversity.com/pages/1631/United-States-SECONDARY-EDUCATION.html**>.

United States. National Center for Education Statistics (NCES). U.S. Department of Education. *Public Elementary and Secondary School Student Enrollment of Staff Counts from the Common Core of Data: School Year 2007 - 2008.* By Amber M. Noel and Jennifer Sable. Institute of Education Sciences, 2009. Web. 12 Nov. 2009. <**www.nces.ed.gov/pubs2010/2010309.pdf**>.

Viadero, Debra. "Education Week: Scholars: Parent-School Ties Should Shift in Teen Years." *Education Week American Education News Site of Record.* Web. 19 Nov. 2009. < **www.edweek.org/ew/articles/2009/11/18/12parent_ep.h29.html**>.

"Weekly Lesson Plan Form: Printable Tool for Teachers (Grades PreK-12) - TeacherVision.com." *Teacher Lesson Plans, Printables & Worksheets by Grade or Subject - TeacherVision.com.* Web. 15 Nov. 2009. <**www.teachervision.fen.com/curriculum-planning/printable/6150.html?detoured=1**>.

Biography

Anne B. Kocsis resides in Camp Hill, Pennsylvania with her husband of 19 years and three kids. She graduated from Dickinson College in Carlisle, Pennsylvania in 1987 with bachelor's degrees in English and German. During her senior year in high school, she said she wanted to be a freelance writer and is now living the dream. Her experience includes technical writing, ghostwriting books, writing freelance articles, editing, writing business proposals, and copywriting. During her spare time, she works on a romance novel and enjoys making jewelry, reading, traveling, and going to the beach. She is also the author of *The Complete Guide to Eco-Friendly House Cleaning: Everything you Need to Know Explained Simply.*

Index

A

B

C

D

E

F

G

I

L

M

N

O

P

R

S

T

W